The 50 String Guitar

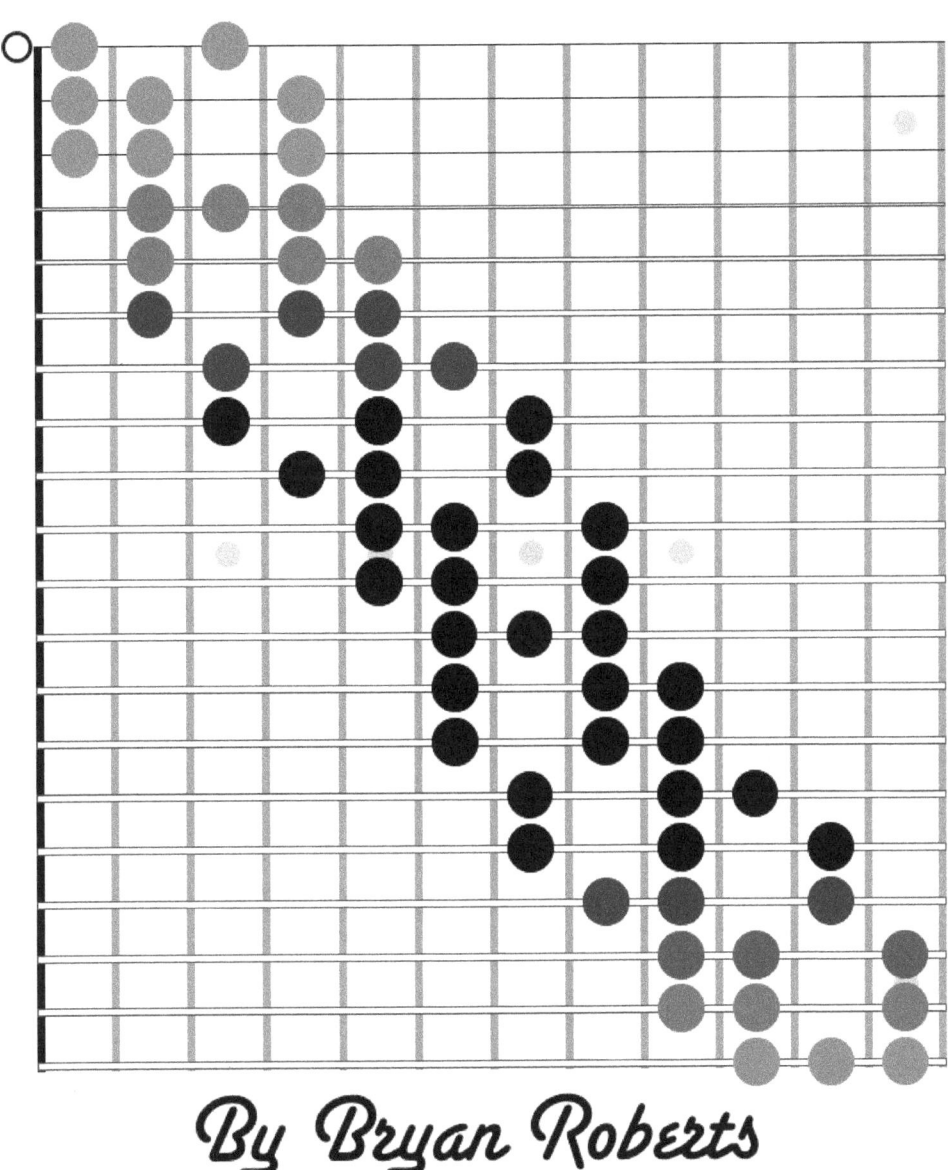

By Bryan Roberts

Copyright © 2013 Bryan Roberts

ISBN: 978-0-9893162-0-0

All rights reserved. No part of this book may be reproduced in any form or by any electronic or mechanical means including information storage and retrieval systems, without the permission in writing of the publisher except by a reviewer who may quote brief passages in a review. Any Unauthorized duplication of this book or its contents is a violation of copyright laws.

Bryan Roberts Publication-West Virginia

Table of Contents

Introduction..1

Basics Shapes...5

    Big Ones, Small Ones, and 134's

Using the 50 String Guitar to Learn the Major Scale..6

Using the 50 String Guitar to Learn the Melodic Minor Scale.....................................11

A New Basic Shape..14

    The Little 3

Using the 50 String Guitar to Learn the Bebop Dominant Scale.................................15

Using the 50 String Guitar to Learn the Bebop Major Scale.......................................19

Two More Basic Shapes...22

    1-2 and 2-1

Using the 50 String Guitar to Learn the Harmonic Minor Scales.................................23

Using the 50 String Guitar to Learn the Harmonic Major Scales.................................27

Using the 50 String Guitar to Learn Pentatonic Scales...29

Using the 50 String Guitar to Learn the Symmetrical Scales......................................34

    1/2 - Whole Diminished with micro structures

    Whole - 1/2 Diminished with micro structures

    Whole Tone Scale

    Augmented Scale with micro structures

Visual Indicators...43

The Modal Number...47

Master Code...49

Modal Comparison...50

Modal Codes..51

Modal Matrices..55

    Major Matrix

    Major Matrix with 7ths

    Melodic Minor Matrix

    Melodic Minor Matrix with 7ths

    Harmonic Minor Matrix

    Harmonic Minor Matrix with 7ths

    Harmonic Major Matrix

    Harmonic Major Matrix with 7ths

Moving Beyond..64

More "Exotic" Scales..65

Appendix:...67

    Fretboard Diagram Key

    The 50 String Guitar

    The Process

        Example 1

    Scale Comparison Chart

    Tradition View Comparison for Pentatonics, Major Scale, Melodic Minor, Harmonic Minor, Harmonic Major, Bebop Dominant, Bebop Major, W/H Diminished, and Whole Tone Scales

    Notes

    Interval Study/Reference

    Blanks for Printing and Study

Introduction

How long would it take you to memorize this?

3.
1415926535897932384626433832795028841971693993751058209
7494459230781640628620899862803482534211706798214808651
3282306647093844609550582231725359408128481117450284102
7019385211055596446229489549303819644288109756659334461
2847564823378678316527120190914564856692346034861045432
6648213393607260249141273724587006606315588174881520920
9628292540917153643678925903600113305305488204665213841
4695194151160943305727036575959195309218611738193261179
3105118548074462379962749567351885752724891227938183011
9491298336733624406566430860213949463952247371907021798
6094370277053921717629317675238467481846766940513200056
8127145263560827785771342757789609173637178721468440901
2249534301465495853710507922796892589235420199561121290
2196086403441815981362977477130996051870721134999999837
2978049951059731732816096318595024459455346908302642522
3082533446850352619311881710100031378387528865875332083
8142061717766914730359825349042875546873115956286388235
3787593751957781857780532171226806613001927876611195909
2164201989380952572010654858632788659361533818279682303
0195203530185296899577362259941389124972177528347913151
5574857242454150695950829533116861727855889075098381754
6374649393192550604009277016711390098488240128583616035
6370766010471018194295559619894676783744944825537977472
6847104047534646208046684259069491293313677028989152104
7521620569660240580381501935112533824300355876402474964
7326391419927260426992279678235478163600934172164121992
4586315030286182974555706749838505494588586926995690927
2107975093029553211653449872027559602364806654991198818
3479775356636980742654252786255181841757467289097777279
3800081647060016145249192173217214772350141441973568548
1613611573525521334757418494684385233239073941433345477
6241686251898356948556209922192221842725502542568876779
0494601653466804988627232791786085784383827967976681454
1009538837863609506800642251252051173929848960841284886
2694560424196528502221066118630674427862203919494504712
3713786960956364371917287467764657573962413890865832645
9958133904780275900994657640789512694683983525957098258
2262052248940772671947826848260147699090264013639443745
5305068203496252451749399651431429809190659250937221696
4615157098583874105978859597729754989301617539284681382
6868386894277415599185592245953959431049972524680845989
7273644695848653836736222626099124608051243884390451244
1365497627807977156914359977001296160894416948685558484.......

We might be here a while. How long to memorize this?

3.141592.....

Much easier right?

You may already know this number as pi and people have actually memorized and recited this number to tens of thousands of digits. I don't have time for that and i'm guessing you probably don't either but let's take a look at that big string of numbers for just a moment. My brain starts to look for patterns immediately. I see areas of contrast where there is less ink used which, to me, looks like clouds within the numbers and I begin to search out repetitive number combinations like 77 or 11. Our brains love a good pattern.

How about this one?

1473625147362514736251473625147362514736251473625147362514736251473625
1473625147362514736251473625147362514736251473625147362514736251473625
1473625147362514736251473625147362514736251473625147362514736251473625
1473625147362514736251473625147362514736251473625147362514736251473625
1473625147362514736251473625147362514736251473625147362514736251473625
1473625147362514736251473625147362514736251473625147362514736251473625
1473625147362514736251473625147362514736251473625147362514736251473625
1473625147362514736251473625147362514736251473625147362514736251473625
1473625147362514736251473625147362514736251473625147362514736251473625
1473625147362514736251473625147362514736251473625147362514736251473625
1473625147362514736251473625147362514736251473625147362514736251473625
1473625147362514736251473625147362514736251473625147362514736251473625
1473625147362514736251473625147362514736251473625147362514736251473625
1473625147362514736251473625147362514736251473625147362514736251473625
1473625147362514736251473625147362514736251473625147362514736251473625..................................

Easy! Just as easy as memorizing this, 1473625. Your brain could immediately pickup the pattern. It's as simple as memorizing a phone number back before cell phones memorized them for you.

For guitarists we have to deal with similar issues.

Can you memorize this?

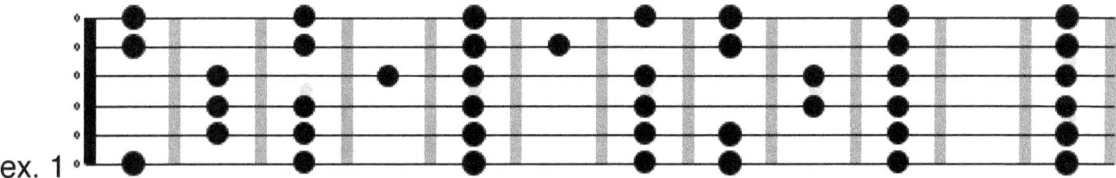
ex. 1

This is the major scale over the whole fretboard and at first glance it is still looks pretty hard to memorize. It can be done, just like pi can be done to a certain number of digits, with hard work and repetition. However it may seem as if there is no easy pattern for the brain to grasp. Well, there is. That means there is a better way!

Is this any better for you?

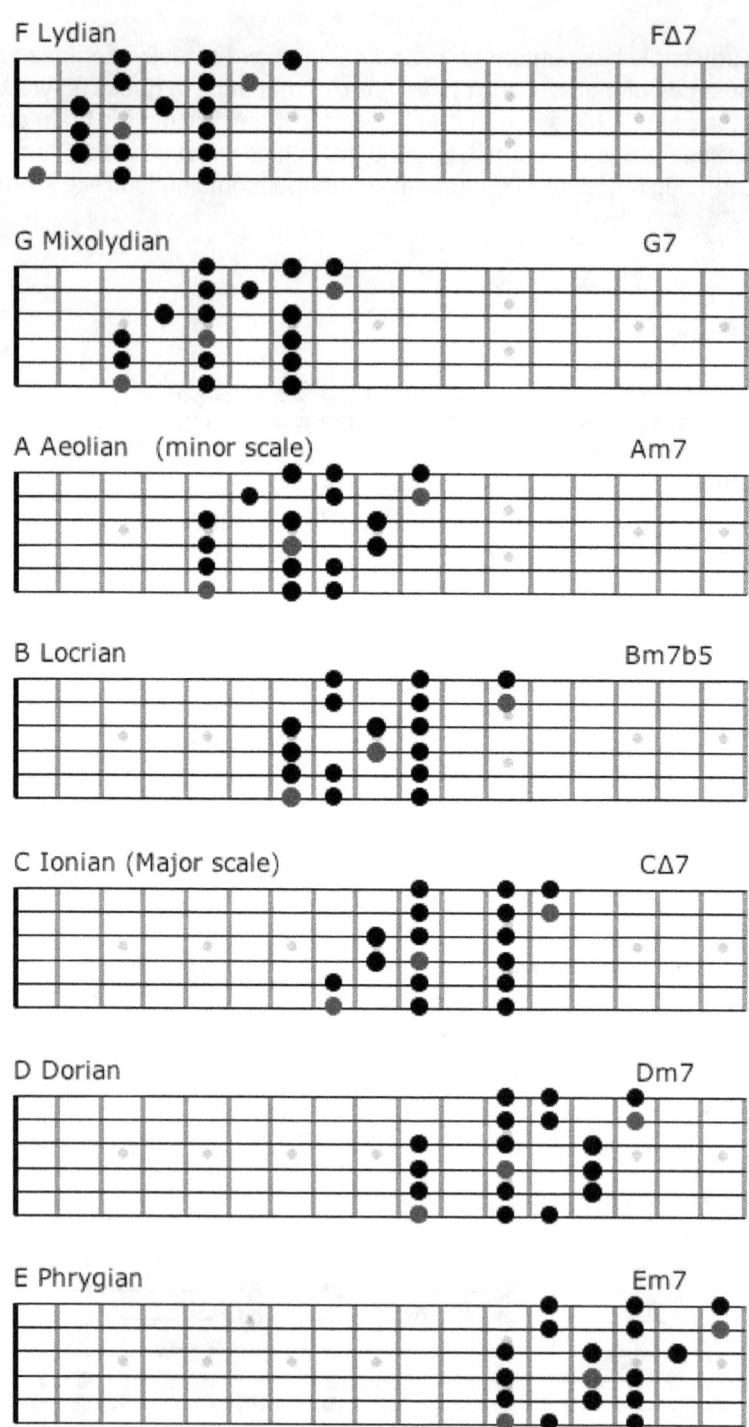

Probably worse right? But this is how the major modes are generally taught. Don't get me wrong, each of these two systems (Ex. 1 & 2) have their place but they will be so much easier after we use the 50 stringed guitar.

And here it is!.......almost.

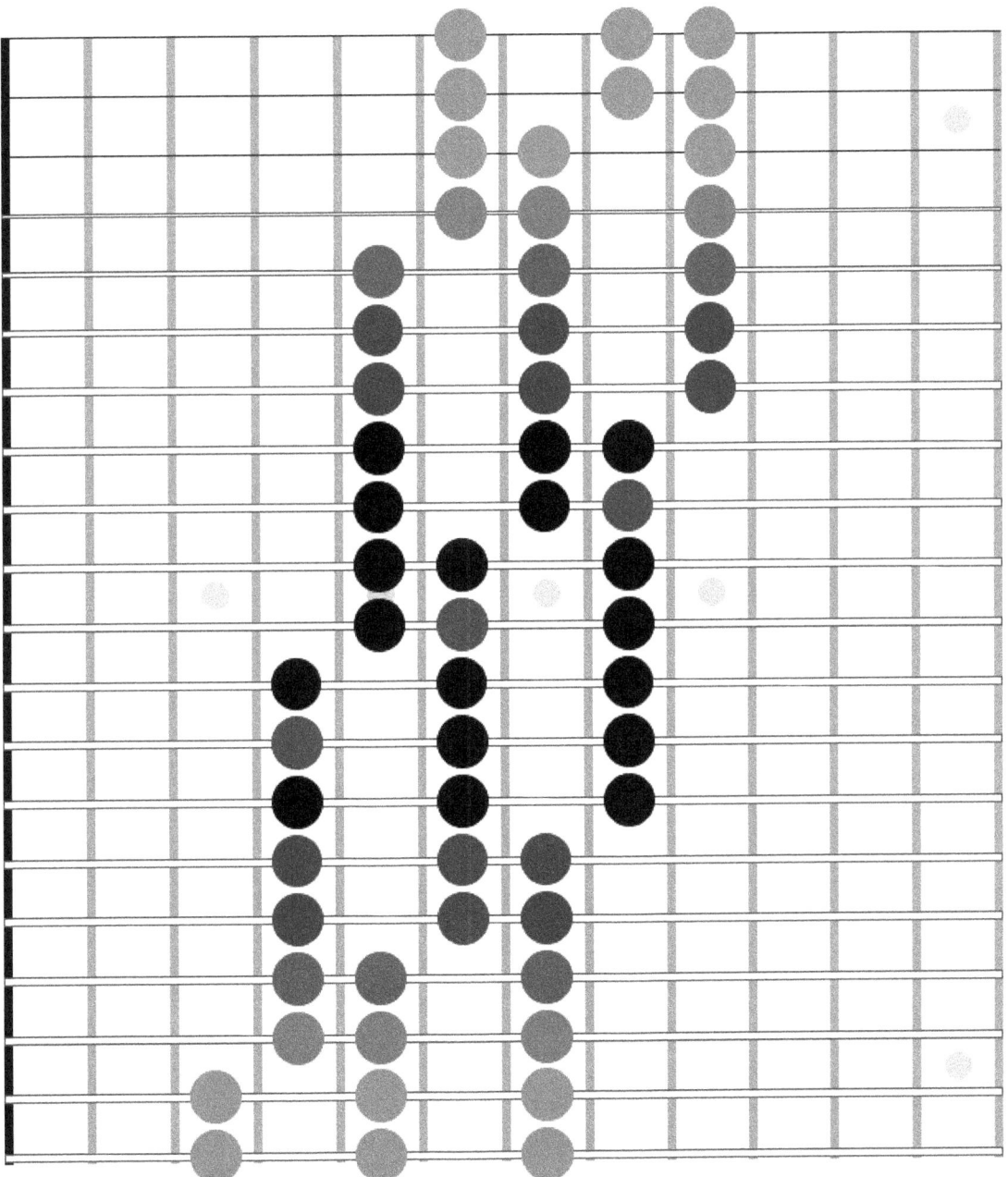

Welcome to the 50 string guitar! This is a my new way of teaching scales and modes that has my students playing every mode of the major scale before the end of a half hour lesson. It works for any scale because it is so much easier on the brain and we are going to make it even easier than it looks here. First we need the basics. So lets imagine a guitar with only 1 string....

Basic Shapes

The Big One

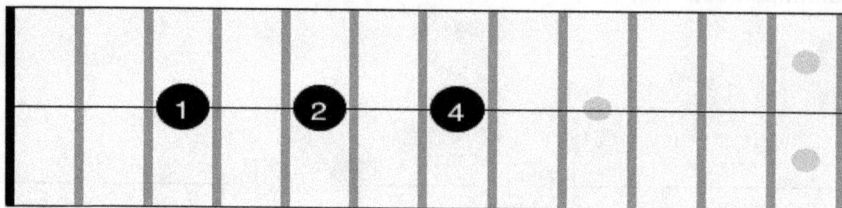

The Small One

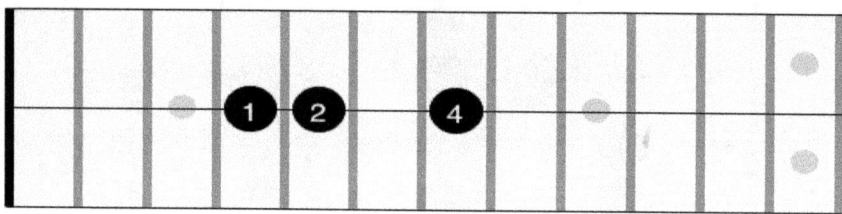

The 134

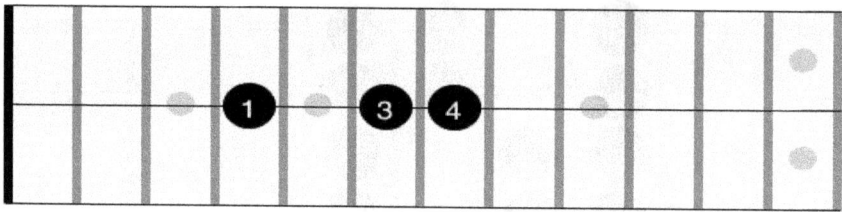

ex. 3

If you're not familiar with fretboard diagrams, go ahead and check the appendix and get that straightened out. Otherwise we should be ready to get started.

On our Unitar (guitar with 1 string) let's play the first basic shape - **The Big One**. Since you probably don't have a real unitar just pick any string on your guitar and play the first fingering shown in example 3. Start by playing finger 1 then 2 then 4 in whole steps beginning on fret 3. You should see why I call this **The Big One**. It is a bit of a stretch for the hand at first but if I can do it you can too. (A little secret...It's all about the thumb. Put it behind the middle finger.)

Play it back and forth, up and down, starting on different frets and different strings. Get to know it...It's **The Big One**. No that's not the technical definition nor will you hear it called that anywhere else but the brain wants names to go with faces to aid in memory.

Ok, easy enough (aside from the **Big** stretch). Let's move on to **The Small One**. Play this one with the same fingers but get rid of that stretch between fingers 1 and 2 that we had in the previous example. There is only a half step between them now. So I call it **The Small One**. It has a **smaller** stretch...genius I know.

And for the final basic shape....**The 134.** The name is even less clever than the others! But you know why I call it that. You do know right? The fingering! Play it in different positions and on different strings just as you did the others. Get to know each basic shape individually. They will be our building blocks as we learn the major and melodic minor scales!

The Major Scale

Now back to the 50 string guitar. This is what the major scale would look like on such a guitar. If we started at the 3rd fret of string 6 (at the bottom of the page) and followed the major scale pattern of whole step - whole step - half step - whole step - whole step - whole step - half step (the old Do, Re, Me, etc..) it would create this fingering pattern on the fretboard.

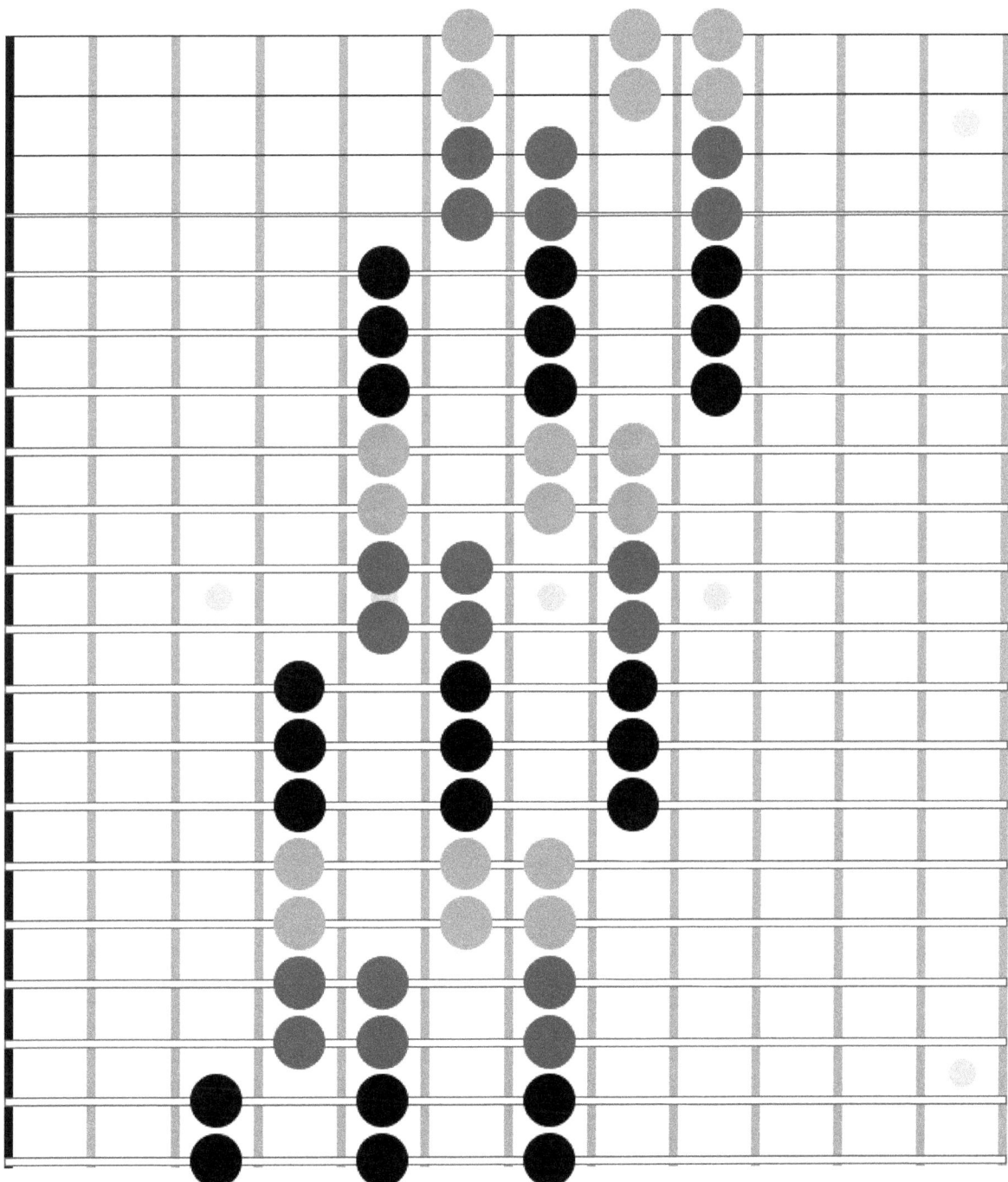

So let's brake this down. The pattern starts with 2 **Big Ones**, then has 2 **Small Ones**, then 2 **134's**. One more **Big One** completes the pattern and then it repeats. So If we look at it continuing on from here we could more easily see it as this...

3 - **Big Ones**

2 - **Small Ones**

2 - **134's**

MEMORIZE THIS!

Find it in the diagram above.

3-Big Ones ------- 2-Small Ones ------------ 2-134's

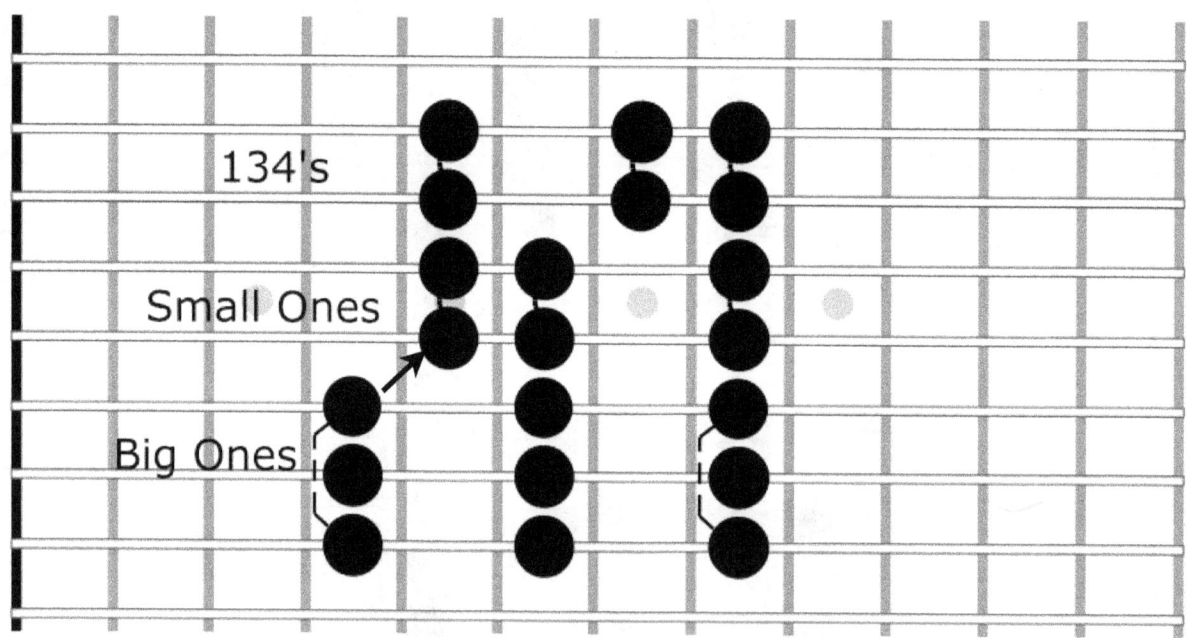

Easy! Now we all we need to do is see how this revolves on a standard 6 string guitar.

Ok, let's start on the F note on the 1st fret of the 6th string. Play the last Big One here. On the next string we move up to the 2nd fret and play the first small one. (In the major scale you always move one fret up after the last Big One. See it in the pattern above?) Continuing through the scale you'll have the last small one on the 4th string. Stay right in line and do the first 134 on the G string. As you get to the 2nd string you have to do what I call **The 2nd String Jump.** This means, for any scale, where ever you are in the pattern you have to move up one fret when you go to the 2nd string.   (This is because of the way your guitar is tuned.) So do the second 134 on the 2nd string starting on the 3rd fret. Finish it up with the first Big One on the high E string.

The pattern continues so what happens when you run out of strings? When you run through the scale to the high E string, simply **repeat the basic shape that you played on the high E string on the same fret of the low E string** and continue on with the pattern. This means that if you played the first Big One on the 3rd fret of the high E string (which we did) you're going to do it again on the 3rd fret of the low E string. That means the second Big One will start on the 3rd fret of the 5th string and so on. As you do this procedure (see The Process in the appendix and search the web for videos by The50StringGuitar for more information) you will work though every mode of the scale going up the neck. Don't forget the Second String Jump!

All you have to remember is..

3 Big Ones
(move one fret forward then do..)
2 Small Ones
2 134's
Do the 2nd String Jump when going to string 2
The Basic Shape played on the high E string repeats on the low E

Ex. 2 in the Introduction should make more sense to you now!

A final note about the scale is needed. You can start anywhere in the pattern but know that **the first note of the 2nd big one is name of the major scale** you're playing. So if you started on the F note at the 1st fret of the 6th string with the 2nd Big One you would be playing the F major scale. If you started on that F note with the *1st Big One* you would be playing the Bb major Scale. Which major scale did we play in the previous example where we started on the last Big One? answer: C Major. To master this you must know where the notes are on the fretboard. (See Notes in the Appendix)

Know this scale inside and out, backwards and forwards, front ways and slantways and all the other ways. It will make all the other scales easier to learn!

Here's a reference for those of you who are having trouble remembering which mode is which.

Major Type	Minor Type
Ionian = begins w/ 2nd Big One--Imaj7	Dorian = begins w/ 2nd 134--ii7
Lydian = begins w/ 3rd Big One--IVmaj7	Phrygian = begins w/ 2nd small one--iii7
Mixolydian = begins w/ 1st Big One--V7	Aeolian = begins w/ 1st 134--vi7
	Locrian = begins w/ 1st small one--vii7b5

Next is the Major Scale on the 50 String Guitar showing the full revolving pattern within the brackets. The numbers indicate the scale degree not the fingering.

Major Scale

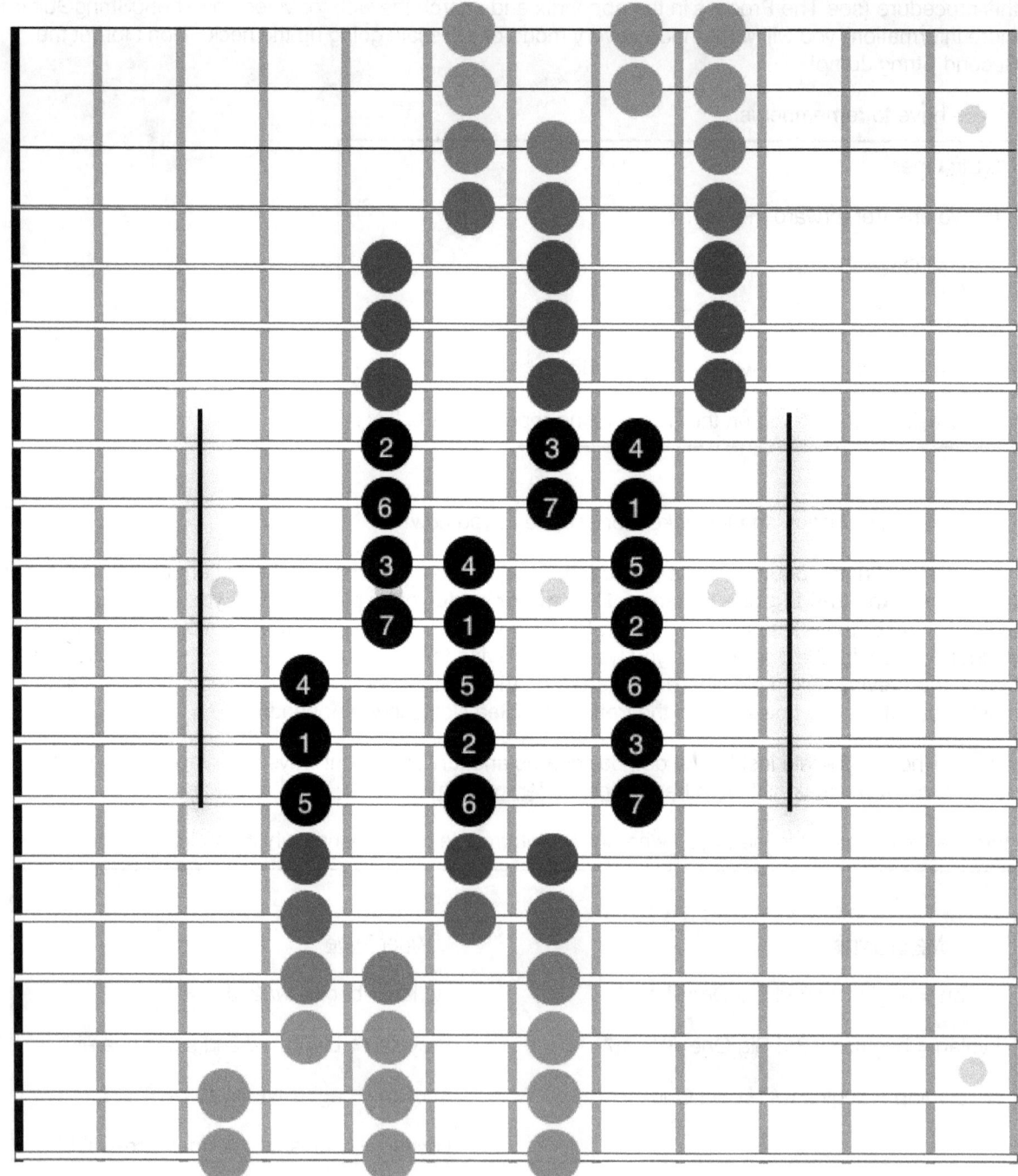

Notes and Ideas

(Use these pages to put down thoughts, licks, and points to remember.)

<u>3 Big ones, 2 Small ones, and 2 134's-------3 Big ones, 2 Small ones, and 2 134's-----------------</u>

Melodic Minor

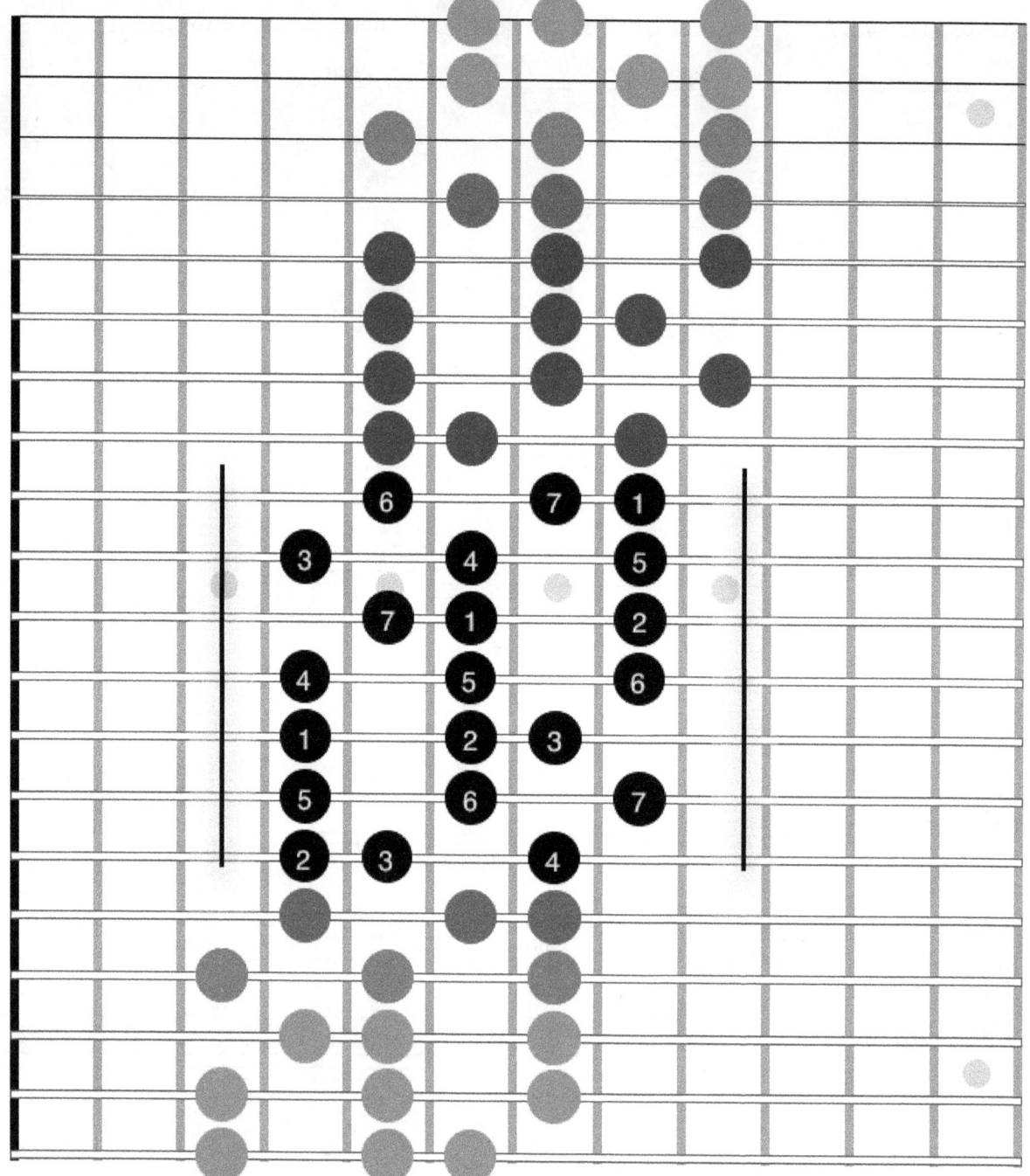

Here is the melodic Minor Scale viewed on the 50 String Guitar. It is a little harder than the major scale but if you're going to use it you're going to be playing more advanced music. Melodic minor is used mostly in jazz, fusion, and classical but not exclusively.   Don't worry if you're not into those styles. Skip ahead to the pentatonic section or...go ahead and get into these styles! This is a great sounding scale so let's dig into it.

This scale still uses our three basic shapes **The Big One, The Small One,** and **The 134.** Here's the order.

```
134
Big One
Small One
Big One
134
Small One
Big One
```

Notice the alternation of **Small Ones** and **The 134's** with **The Big One** in between. In fact if we look at it starting with the 2nd degree we'll see a pattern that is easier to remember.

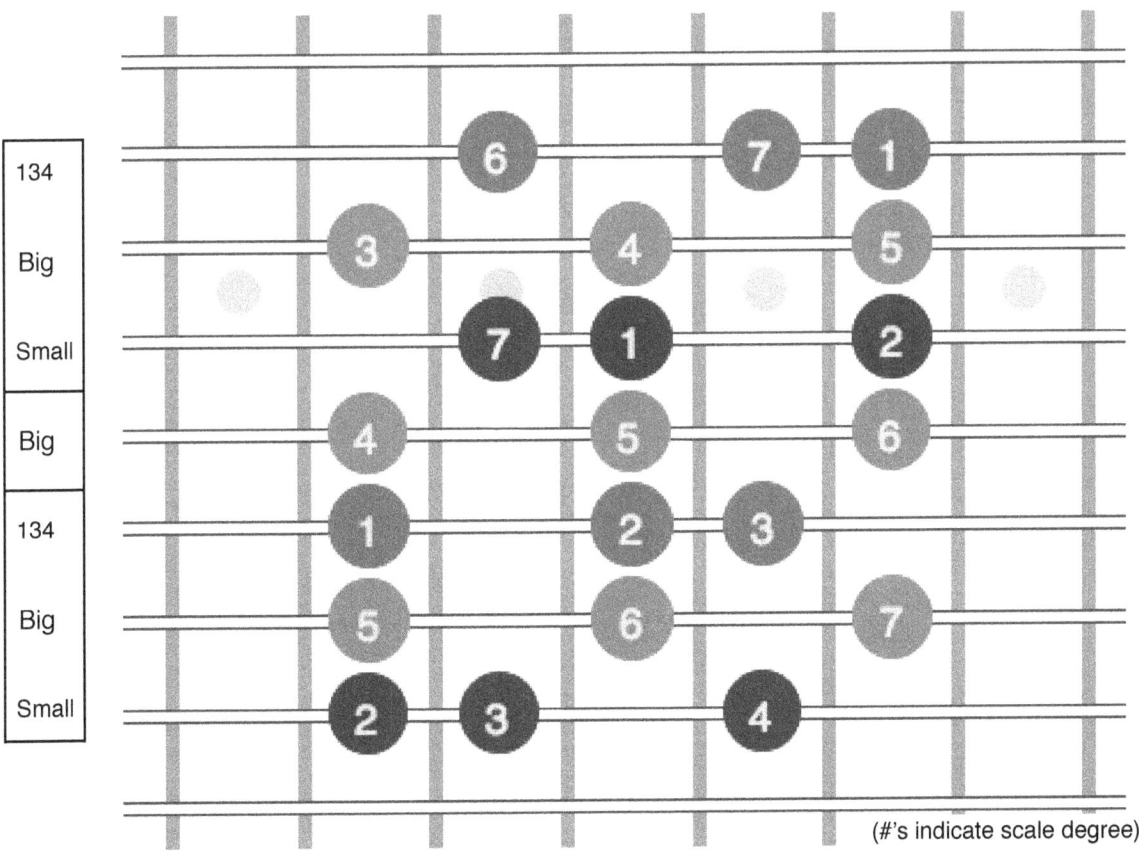

(#'s indicate scale degree)

Just to make sure you know how to do this let's go through a practice run. We are going to play the F Melodic Minor Scale. This means you have to start with the 1st degree of the scale on an F note. So we will use the F note on the 1st fret of string 6 and play the 134 that begins the scale. String 5 will have a Big One at fret one. Move to fret two of the D string and play a small one. The G string will have a Big One on fret 1. Now we will have to jump up two frets on the B string. Why? We're on the second string so we must do the **2nd String Jump.** Then there's the natural jump forward within the pattern itself at this point. (Check out the example above above.) Finally we have a small one on string 1.

What do we do now? Yep..**repeat the basic shape that you played on the high E string on same fret of the low E string** and continue on with the pattern. Then do it again when you've run through the pattern and get to the high E string.. and again.. and again.. and again.. and again.. and again.. and now you will have played all of the modes of the F Melodic Minor Scale.

What about a reference for this scale. Well now you should notice (or be pointed to the fact) that all minor type scales must start with either a 134 or a small one. So far, all major type scales start with a Big One. Scales that we have looked at so far that I consider minor type scales would be Dorian, Phrygian, and Aeolian (natural minor) from the major scale and modes 1, 2, 6, and 7 of Melodic minor.

I believe the easiest way to know melodic minor is to compare it to the major modes. The common names for the modes of melodic minor should be reconsidered I believe.

Mode 1 -------Melodic Minor (minor = b3, melodic = having or producing melody?)

Mode 2 -------Dorian b9 (ok b9 makes sense Dorian must mean b3 and b7)

Mode 3 -------Lydian Augmented (Lydian means #4 and augmented means #5)

Mode 4 -------Lydian Dominant (#4 and Dominant must mean b7 here)

Mode 5 -------Mixolydian b6 (Mixolydian means b7, b6 makes sense)

Mode 6 -------Semilocrian (almost Locrian?)

Mode 7 -------Superlocrian (more than Locrian or like Locrian but awesome?)

There is very little logic in this naming system and it is too complicated. I believe Mixolydian b6 make the most sense. Therefor I propose we use this naming system....

```
Mode 1 -------Ionian b3

Mode 2 -------Dorian b2

Mode 3 -------Phrygian b1

Mode 4 -------Lydian b7

Mode 5 -------Mixolydian b6

Mode 6 -------Aeolian b5

Mode 7 -------Locrian b4
```

Easy enough? The Greek names represent the mode number and the alterations, when compared to the major modes, have a nice easy order. Logic. There are some arguments to be made against these names but in the end I believe this is the best system. If you learn the major modes first, as most students do, you will have an easier time with this system. If you already know Ionian, you just need to flatten the 3rd degree to get melodic minor. If you already know the Dorian mode of the major scale simply flatten the 2nd note to get the second mode of melodic minor.   It's only one note different. It's like learning the C major scale then moving on to the G major scale. No problem, just change one note.

In the following chapter we will look at some other scales that use a new basic shape along with the old ones. I'll call the new one the **Little 3** and with its addition into our arsenal we can begin to learn the Bebop Scales!

Here's our new basic shape shown on the Unitar.

The Little 3

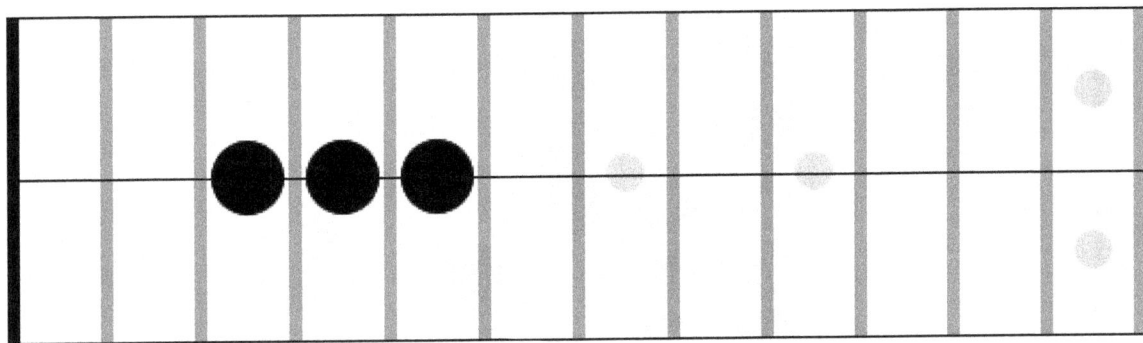

It is simply three notes in a row. Easy as 1 2 3!

Notes and Ideas

Bebop Dominant

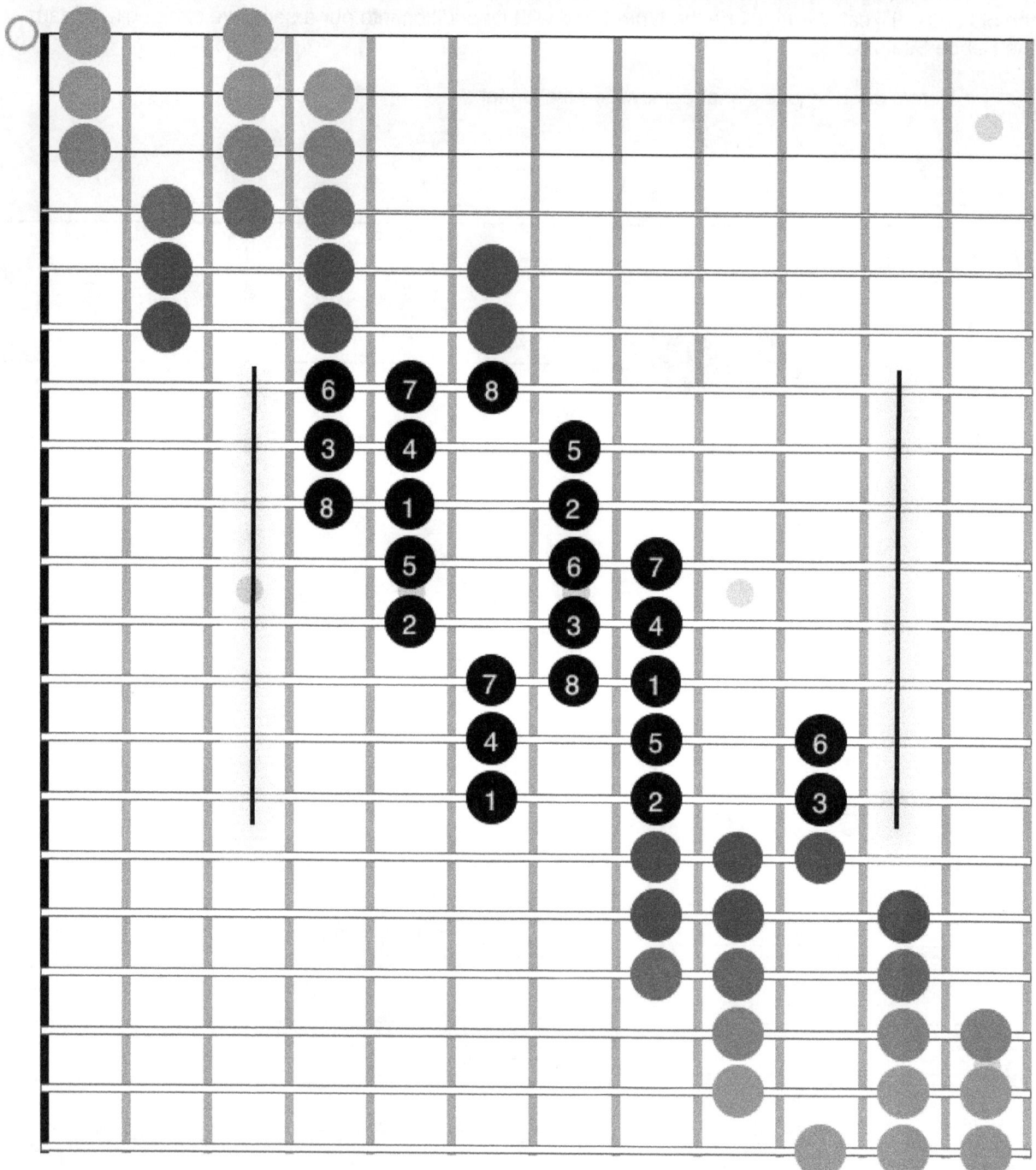

The Bebop Dominant Scale is an eight note scale. It is basically Mixolydian with an added natural 7th degree. Why? David Baker has written extensively about the Bebop Scales and there usage. I encourage those of you who are interested to get his book series. The 50 String Guitar really isn't a "licks" or "theory" book. It is a 'brain-easy' way to learn the scale patterns on the fretboard. Then you can make your own licks.

So a study of the 50 String Guitar above will reveal its repeating pattern and a nice symmetry for your brain to enjoy.

> 2 - **Big Ones**
>
> A **Little 3**
>
> 2 - **134's**
>
> 2 - **Small Ones**
>
> A **Little 3**

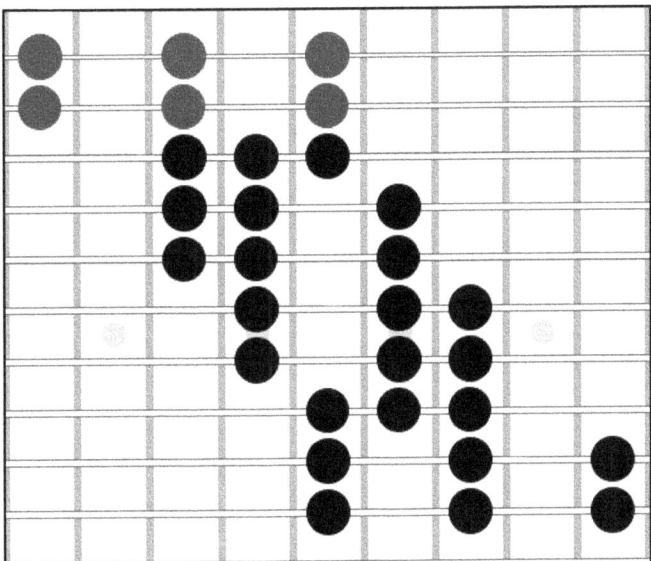

You may also notice that this scale works its way back diagonally as you go up in pitch. This is different than the Major and Melodic Minor scales we did earlier. Therefor we should start the Bebop Scales high on the neck because each new cycle will bring us closer to the open strings. Let's try it out with E Bebop Dominant.

Starting on the 12th fret play 2 **Big Ones**. One on string 6 and the next on string 5. Now it's time for our new basic shape, the **Little 3**. It will be played at the 12th fret of string 4. Next play the two **134's**. The first on fret 11 of string 3 and the next on fret 12 of string 2. (Remember the 2nd String Jump!?) Now play the first **Small One** on string 1, fret 11.

Now it's time to cycle up to the sixth string again. We ended the last mode with the first **Small One** so we will take it up to the sixth string and <u>do it again</u> in the same fret (the 11th). Next, do the 2nd **Small One** on string 5, fret 11. Now it's time for the another **Little 3** on string 4, fret 11. Jump back two frets and start the Bebop Dominant pattern over with the 1st **Big One** on fret 9 of string 3. Do a **2nd String Jump** to fret 10 and play the next **Big One** on string 2. Next is the **Little 3** on string 1, fret 10. What now?

Yep.. **repeat the basic shape that you played on the high E string on same fret of the low E string** and continue on with the pattern. Then do it again when you've run through the pattern and get to the high E string.. and again.. and again.. and again.. and again.. and again.. until you have played all of the modes of the Bebop Dominant Scale.

By now you should be getting to know how the process works. But you also need to do it in reverse, be able to shift up and down the string, start on different frets and strings within the modal shapes. Get to work, nobody's going to do it for you! If you need more help, study **The Process** in the appendix and search the web for upcoming videos by The50StringGuitar.

What about names? I really enjoy the names for the modes of the Bebop Dominant Scale And they make sense if you know the Major Modes really well but I will offer another way to look at them.

Traditional Names	Brain Easy Names
Mixionian	Mixolydian + Δ7th
Doriolian	Aeolian + Δ6th
Phrygiolocrian	Locrian + perfect 5th
Lydionian	Ionian + #4th
Mixodorian	Dorian + Δ3rd
Phrygiolian	Phrygian + Δ2
Lydiocrian	Lydian + #1
Locrydian	Supertasticawesomeleadtonelocrian

You can also view these scales as *the major modes plus a note* as my names indicate. Here's an example. Which notes indicate the added 'bebop note' to the Ionian mode? If you have learned the major modes very well this shouldn't be a problem. Your brain might see this example as C Ionian + C Lydian.

C Ionian + #4

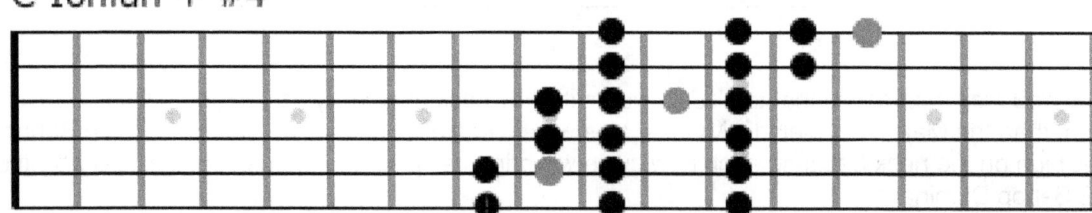

In the next section we'll look at Bebop Major. It will be using the same four basic shapes.

Notes and Ideas

<u>Why use a "bebop note"? One reason is that it can keep the chord tones on the down beat.</u>

<u>What else can it do? Write down some Bebop licks below.</u>

Bebop Major

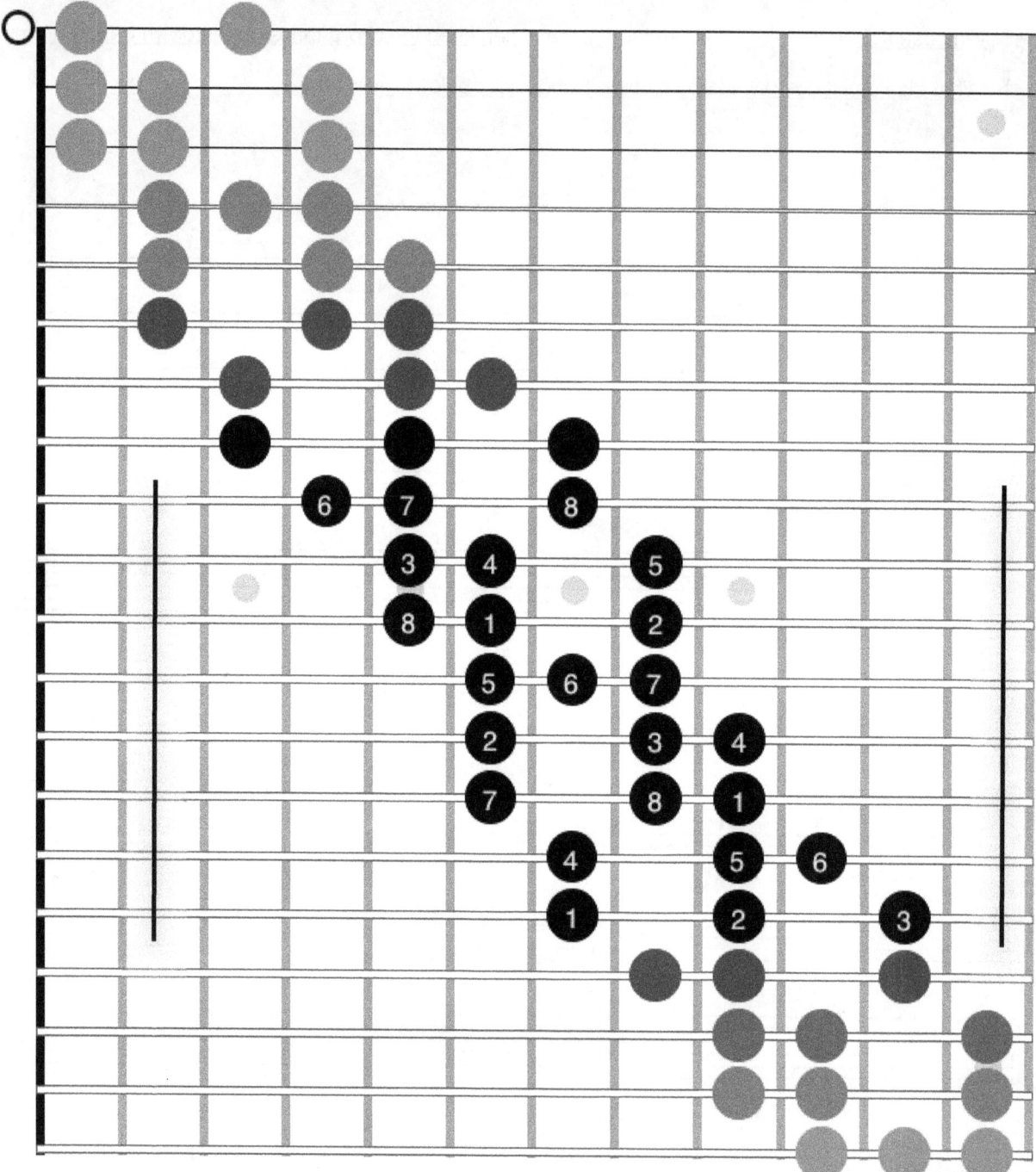

By now you should know how this works so I'm just going to give you the breakdown and let you get to work. Go on...get to work.

A **Big One**

3 -**134's** (watch that jump back after the 1st one)

A **Little 3**

3 **Small Ones** (watch the jump on the last one)

!!Remember the **2nd String Jump**!!

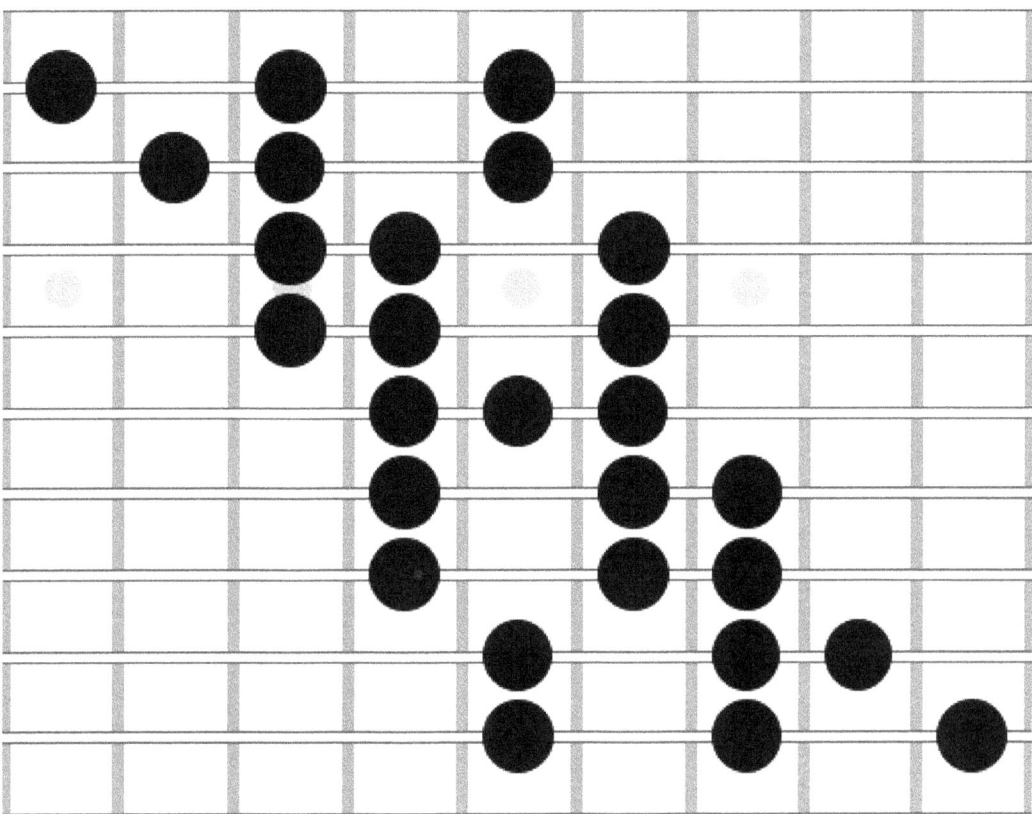

Major Bebop - Ionian + #5

Dorian Blues - Dorian + #4

Phrygian Bebop - Phrygian + Δ3

Lydian Minor Bebop - Lydian + #2

Mixolydian add b9 - Mixolydian + #1

Diminished Augmented - ok

Harmonic Minor Bebop - Aeolian + Δ7

Locrian Diminished Bebop - Locrian + Δ6

Notes and Ideas

Could the "bebop note" be placed in other places within the Major Scale? YES

Could it be placed in other scales like melodic and harmonic minor? YES

Write them below and on the blanks in the index then USE THEM!

More Basic Shapes
for Harmonic Scales

The 1-2

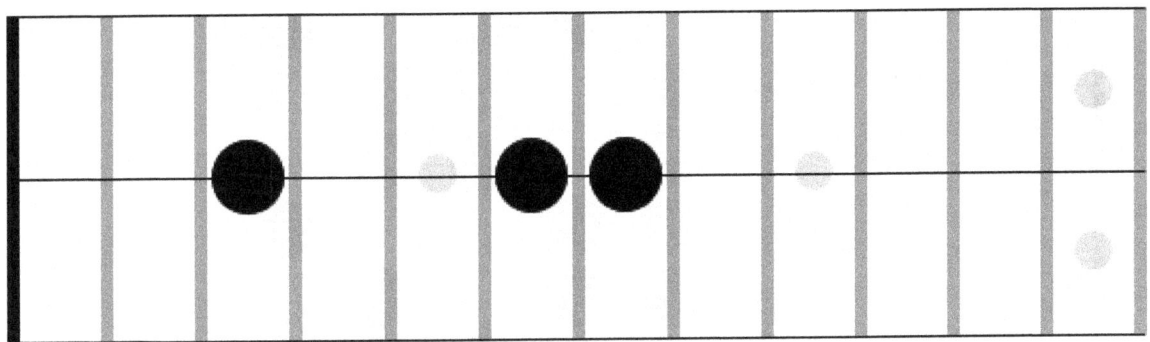

The 2-1

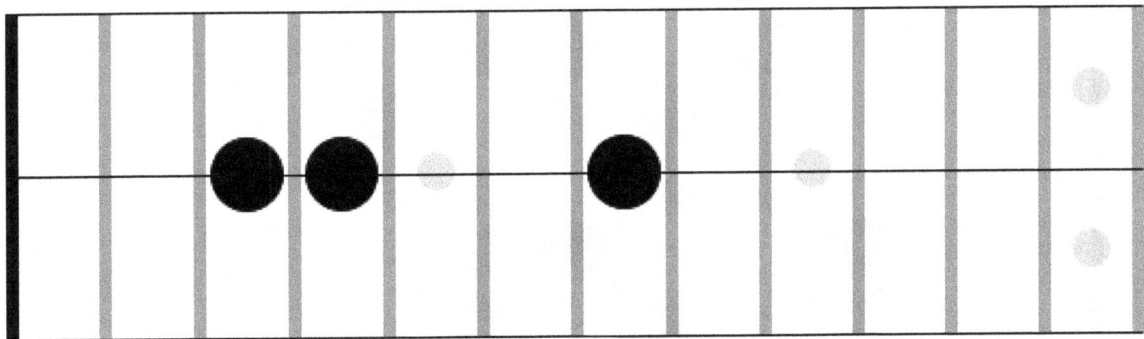

Time to introduce a few more basic shapes. Say hello to the **1-2** and its mirror image the **2-1**. Ahhh, symmetry. These will be used with our first three basic shapes to make the Harmonic Minor and Harmonic Major Scales.

Harmonic Minor

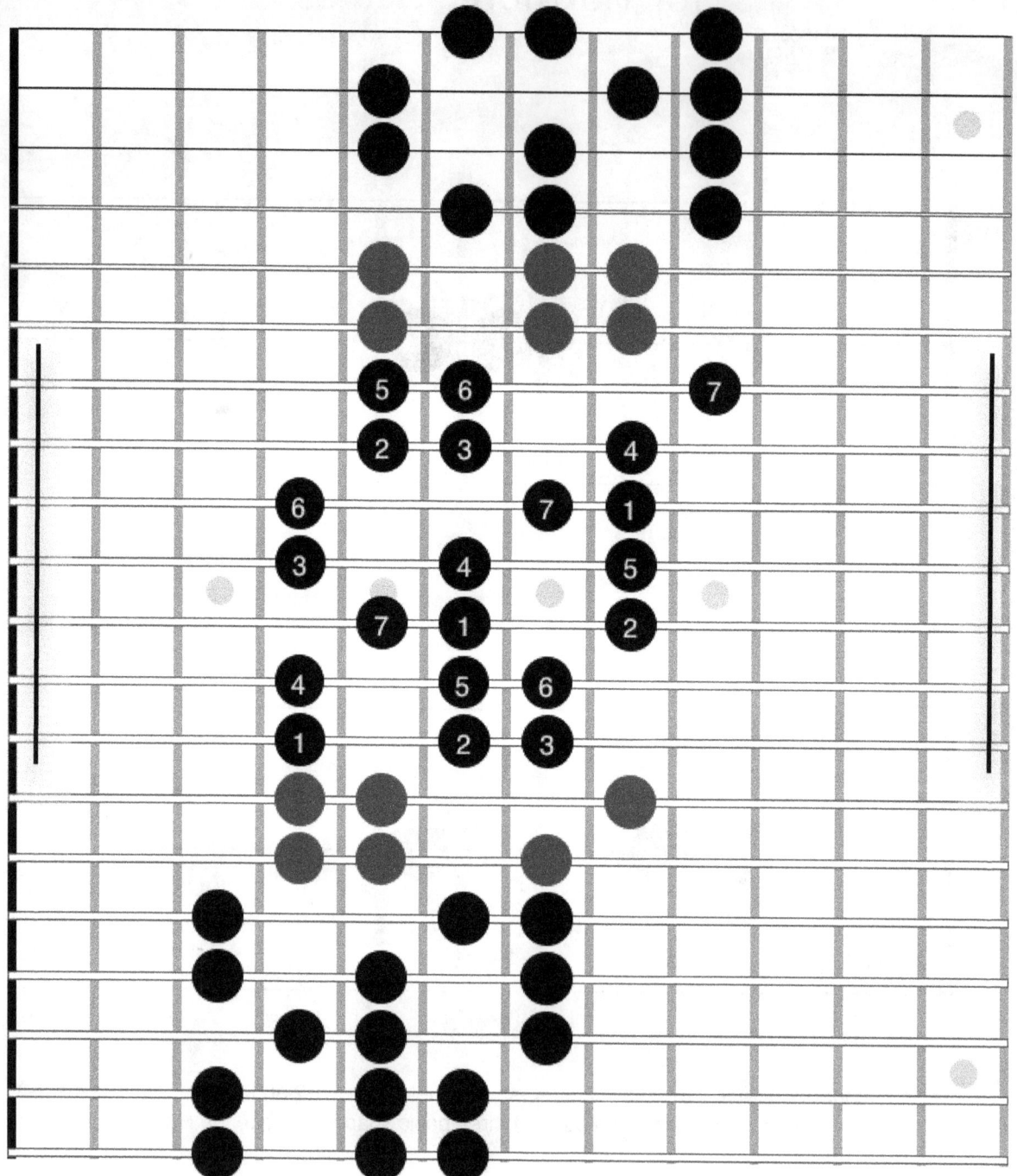

The Harmonic Minor Scale os a seven note scale that is widely used. It is simply the Major scales 6th mode Aeolian with a raised 7th degree. Go ahead and compare them on the 50 stringed guitar and observe that only one note has changed. This makes naming the modes easy.

Aeolian #7
Locrian #6
Ionian #5
Dorian #4
Phrygian #3
Lydian #2
Mixolydian #1

Can we just go ahead and forget the old mode names already? Romanian, Phrygian Dominant (Spanish Gypsy), Ultralocrian?!!? Come on, really? These might be great for those people who want to sound exotic but for those of us that just want to make sense of this thing called music...we don't need any more confusion.

Here's a short view of the Harmonic Minor Scale with its basic shapes.

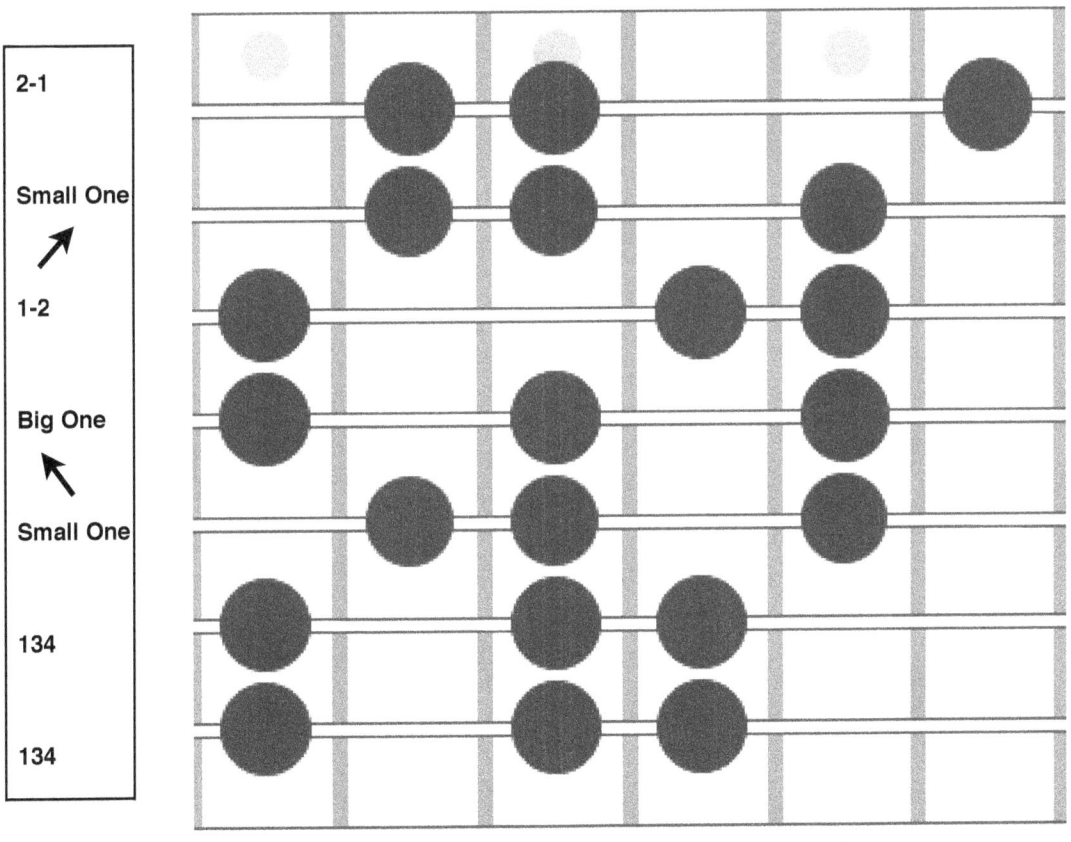

Harmonic Minor may seem a little more complicated because you are dealing with 5 Basic shapes. If you think of it as Aeolian with a # every seven notes it is somewhat easier. When thinking this way, and by studying the chart, you'll see that compared to Aeolian the first and last **Big Ones** are distorted. The same is true for the second **Small One**. The *first* note of the 1st **Big One** is #(sharp). The *second* note of the 2nd **Big One** is #. The *third* note of the 2nd **Small One** is #.

Another interesting feature your brain may have noticed is the diagonal line of notes. In the Harmonic Minor scale above the diagonal lines indicate that there is a series of minor 3rd intervals within the scale and a sign of the diminished 7th chord. If there is only one row of diagonal notes on the 50 string guitar fretboard diagram, such as on the Major scale, it is a sign of the the half diminished chord (m7b5). A study of Melodic Minors fretboard diagram would reveal two diagonal lines of note a whole step apart. This is a visual indication of the augmented chord that exists within that scale. We'll talk more about visual indications later.

Major Scale

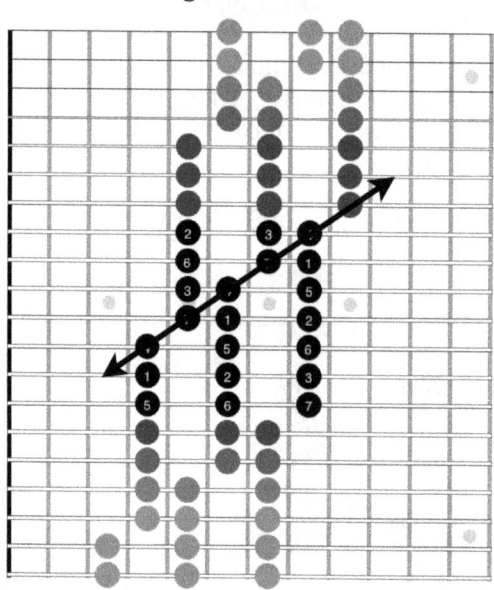

Harmonic Minor

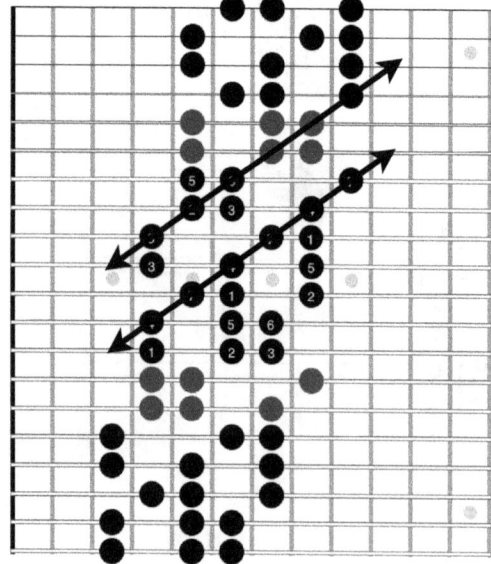

Melodic Minor

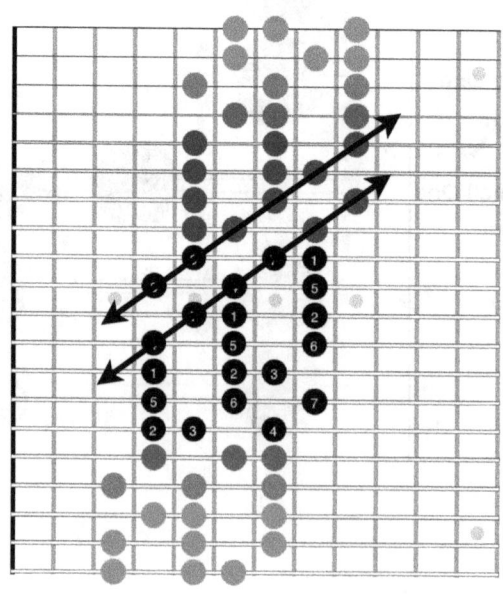

Notes and Ideas

Harmonic Major

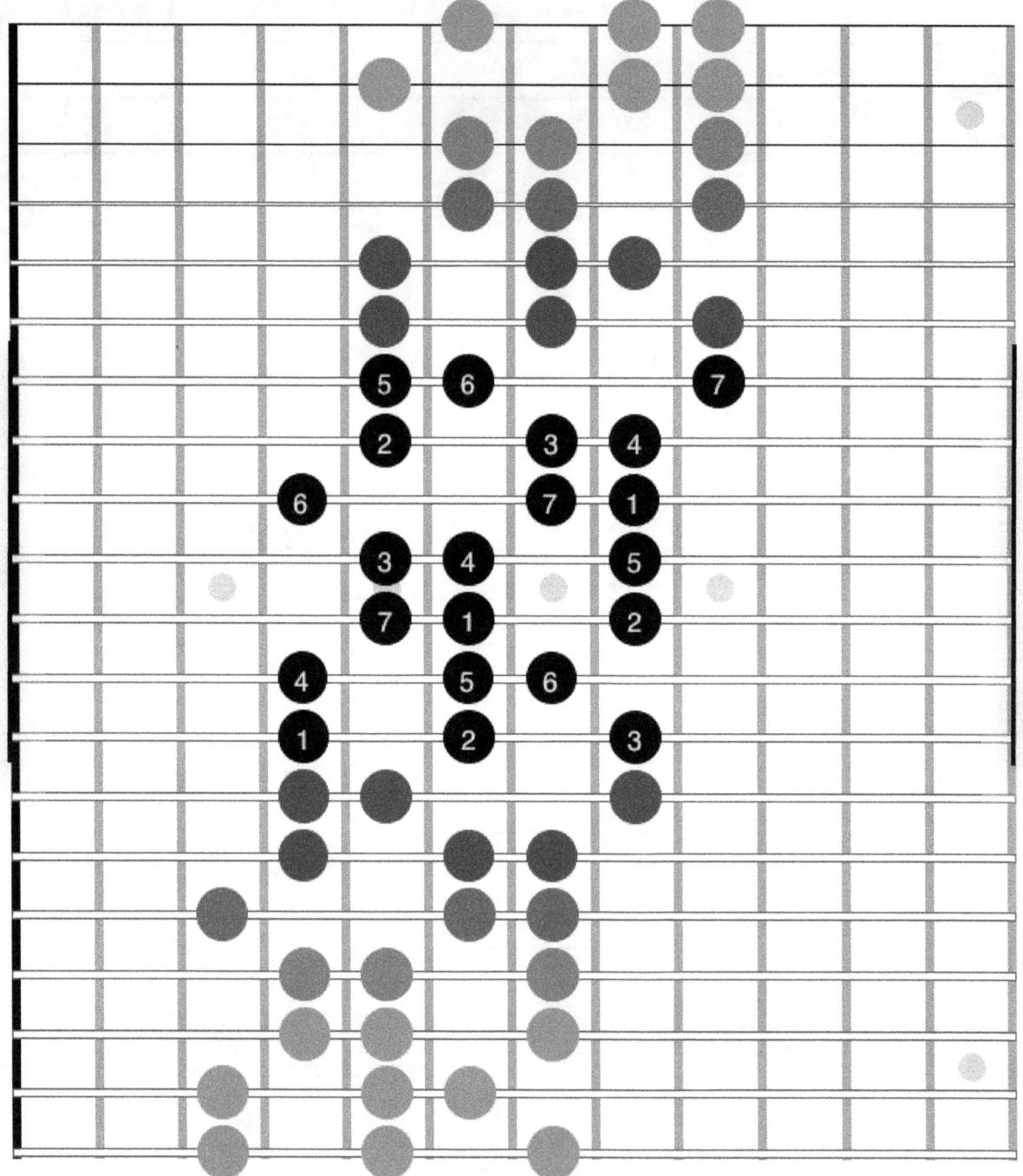

Here's Harmonic Major. It is a scale that many students simply don't get to in their study because the traditional way of learning scales takes so long. If you've worked through this book you should be able to handle it. Let's see what you've learned.

1. What basic shapes are used in this scale?

2. What is the order of basic shapes from lowest to highest?

3. What would be the simplest names for the modes of this scale?

4. Any distinguishing features?

Answers.

5. Big Ones, 134's, Small Ones, 1-2's and 2-1's.

6. The order starting with the string 6 is...a Big One, a 134, 2 Small Ones, a 1-2, a 134, and a 2-1.

7. Ionian b6, Dorian b5, Phrygian b4, Lydian b3, Mixolydian b2, Aeolian b1, Locrian b7.

8. Yes. The diagonals indicate the existence of the diminished 7th chord in this scale. The *first* note of the 1st 134 is flat. The *second* note of the 1st Big One is flat. The *third* note of the last Big One is flat.

Notes and Ideas

Minor/Major Pentatonic

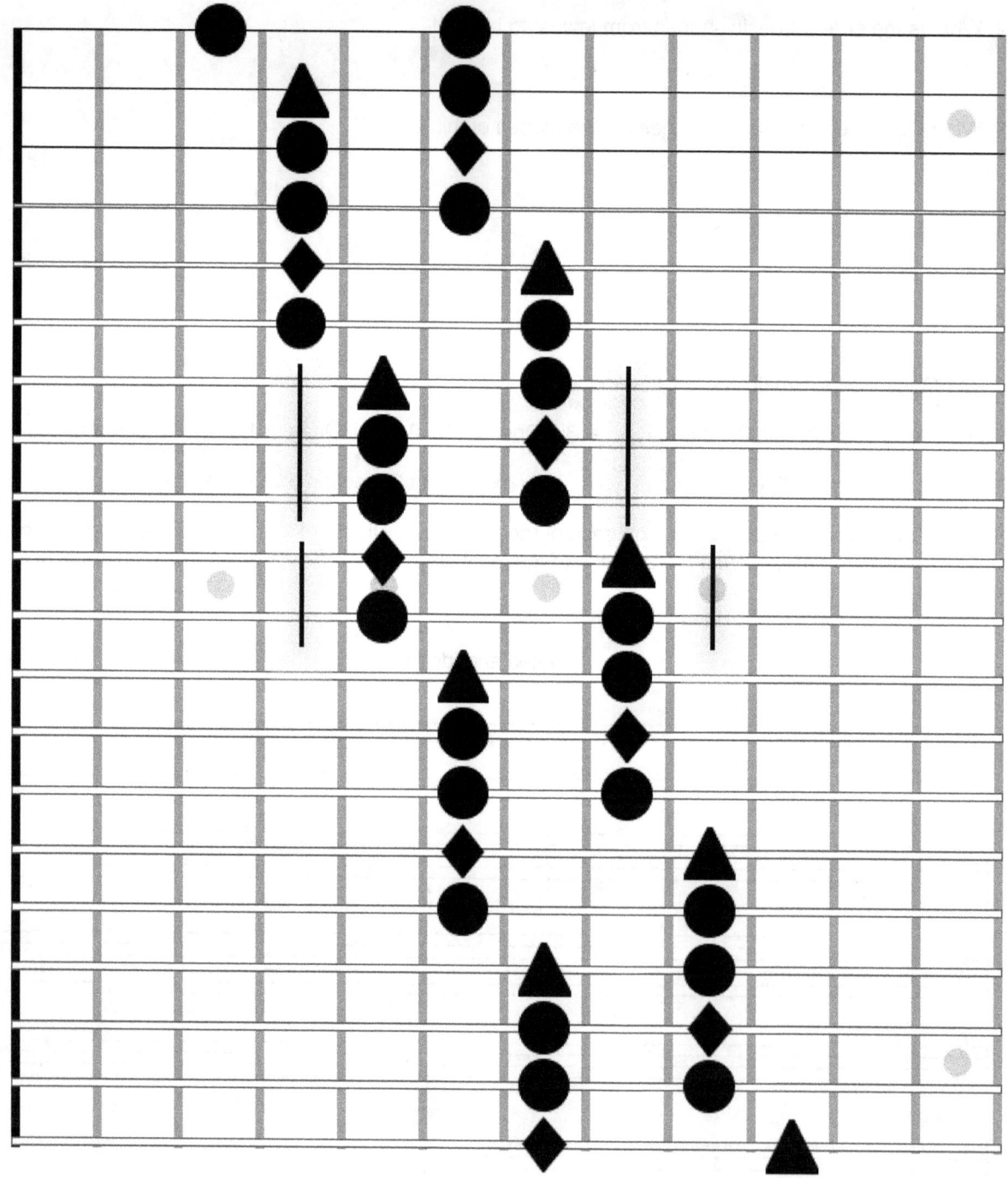

The Pentatonic Scale is a five note scale (penta) that is probably the most widely used improvisational device for guitarists and for good reason. It is easy and it introduces the student and the audience to non-chord tones without excess tension. Since it only has five notes it will operate differently on the 50 String Guitar (and on the 6 string). Its basic shapes do not have three notes, only two, and when you revolve the pattern as we have with the previous scales on the 6 string guitar you would be forced into looping the same box shape over and over. Nevertheless, viewing the pentatonic scale on the 50 String Guitar will allow you to grasp its overall pattern and therefor learn its box shapes more easily.

The Diamond shape indicates the Minor Pentatonic and the Triangle indicates the Major Pentatonic. Yes they're basically the same thing but they are named two different things. More confusion for the student I know. I like to consider it a single scale that works over more than one chord. The pentatonic above would work nicely over a Bm chord and/or over a D major chord. Remember everything is movable on the guitar so say we put the diamond on a G note, we would be playing a scale that works over a Gm or a Bb Major. If we put the *triangle* on an A note the scale would play nicely with an A Major and a F#m chord. This is by no means the extent of the pentatonics' usage.

Five notes in the scale.........

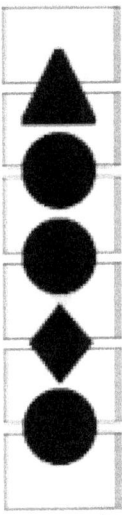

..........hmmm, interesting.

Since there are five notes there are five modes or box shapes. The main box shape should be the one that has both the minor and major indicators on the sixth string. It is most useful and the most taught. The other boxes radiate out from that. In other words, they extend up and down the guitar neck. The next page shows these boxes.

As we have learned, string one is the same as string six on the standard guitar. They are both E's. So here we should be able to see how the boxes revolve on the six string. Remember the **2nd string Jump**!

Check it out.

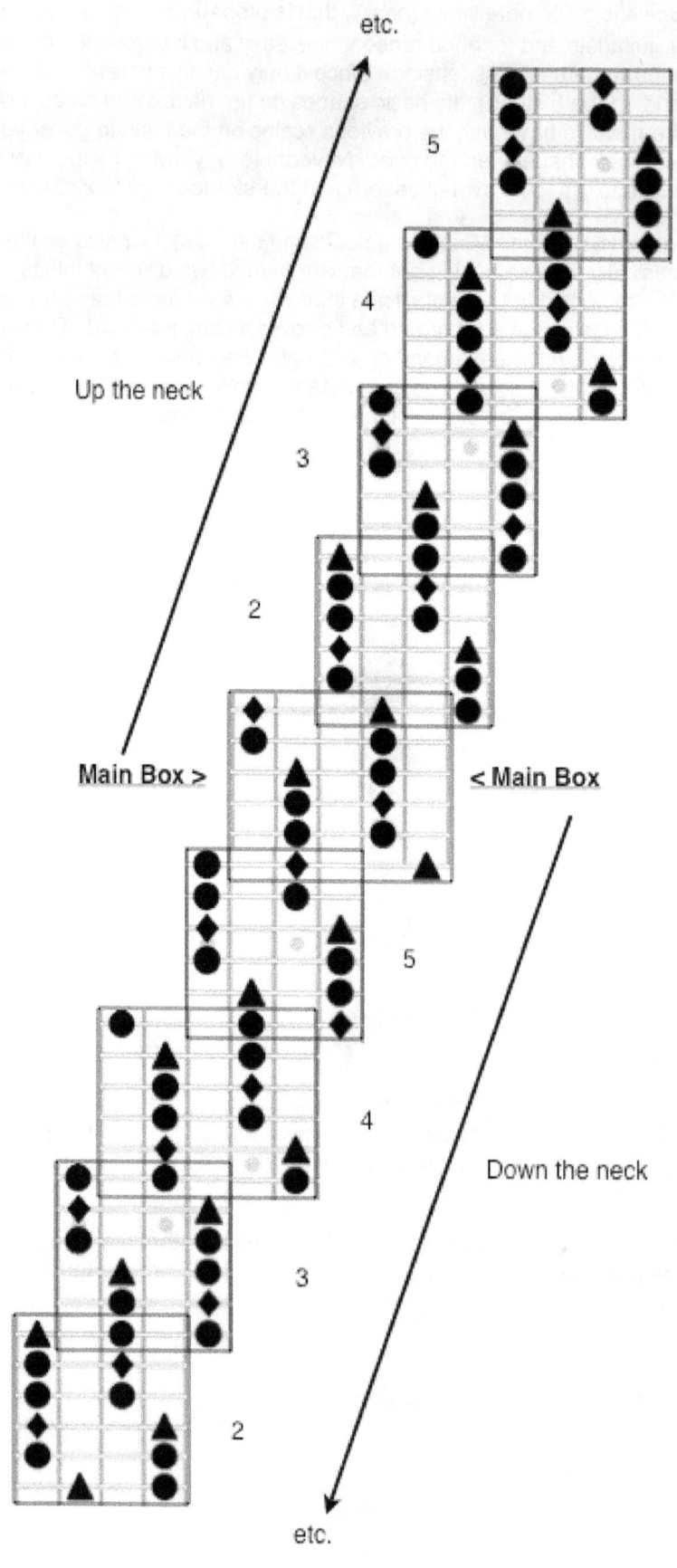

Be sure to break this down. Notice the basic shapes for the pentatonic scale. There are two.

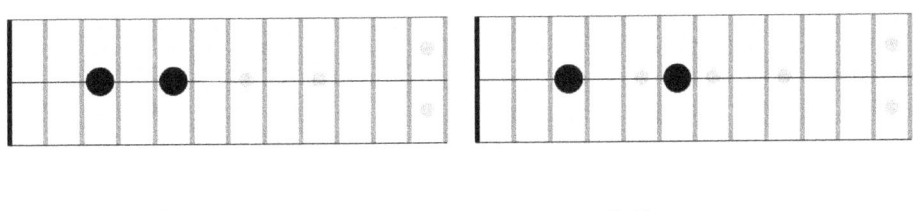

1-3's   1-4's

> Main Box starts with last 1-4
>
> Box 2 stars with last 1-3
>
> Box 3 starts with first 1-3
>
> Box 4 starts with first 1-4
>
> Box 5 starts with middle 1-3

Remember, you don't have to memorize all of those boxes. Learn the full pattern from the 50 String Guitar...

> 2 1-4's
>
> 3 1-3's
>
> Jump back a fret and repeat

Know where your roots are (the minor diamond and the major triangle on the 2nd of the 1-4's). Know how it revolves on the 6 string. Start revolving it on the 6 string guitar!

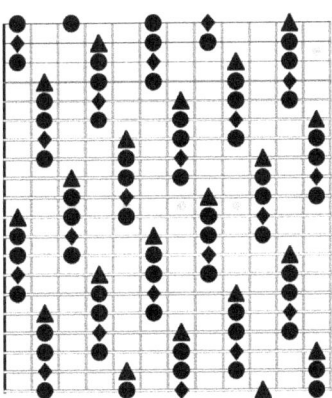

*In the Appendix I have included a traditional view of the pentatonic scale for comparison and study.

Notes and Ideas

Symmetrical Scales

Symmetrical scales are actually fairly easy to learn. Their patterns are repetitive and easy to see. They have the property of limited transposition. This means that, unlike the previous scales in this book, the symmetrical scales become repetitive before twelve frets. In the case of the whole tone scale the notes begin to repeat themselves after two frets so the A whole tone scale has the same notes as the B whole tone scale which has the same notes as the C# whole tone scale and so on. The symmetrical scales also have either six, hexatonic, or eight, octatonic, notes. Each has an interesting and easily recognizable sound. Don't forget the **2nd String Jump**!

Augmented Scale

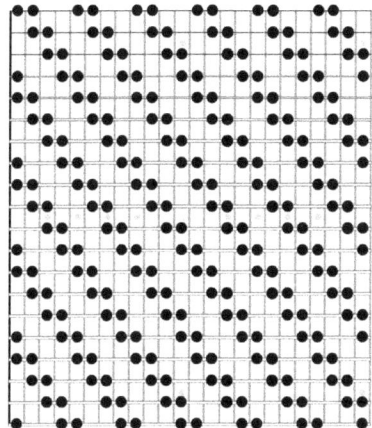

Whole Tone Scale

1/2-Whole Diminished

Whole-1/2 Diminished

Ex. 4

Whole-1/2 Diminished

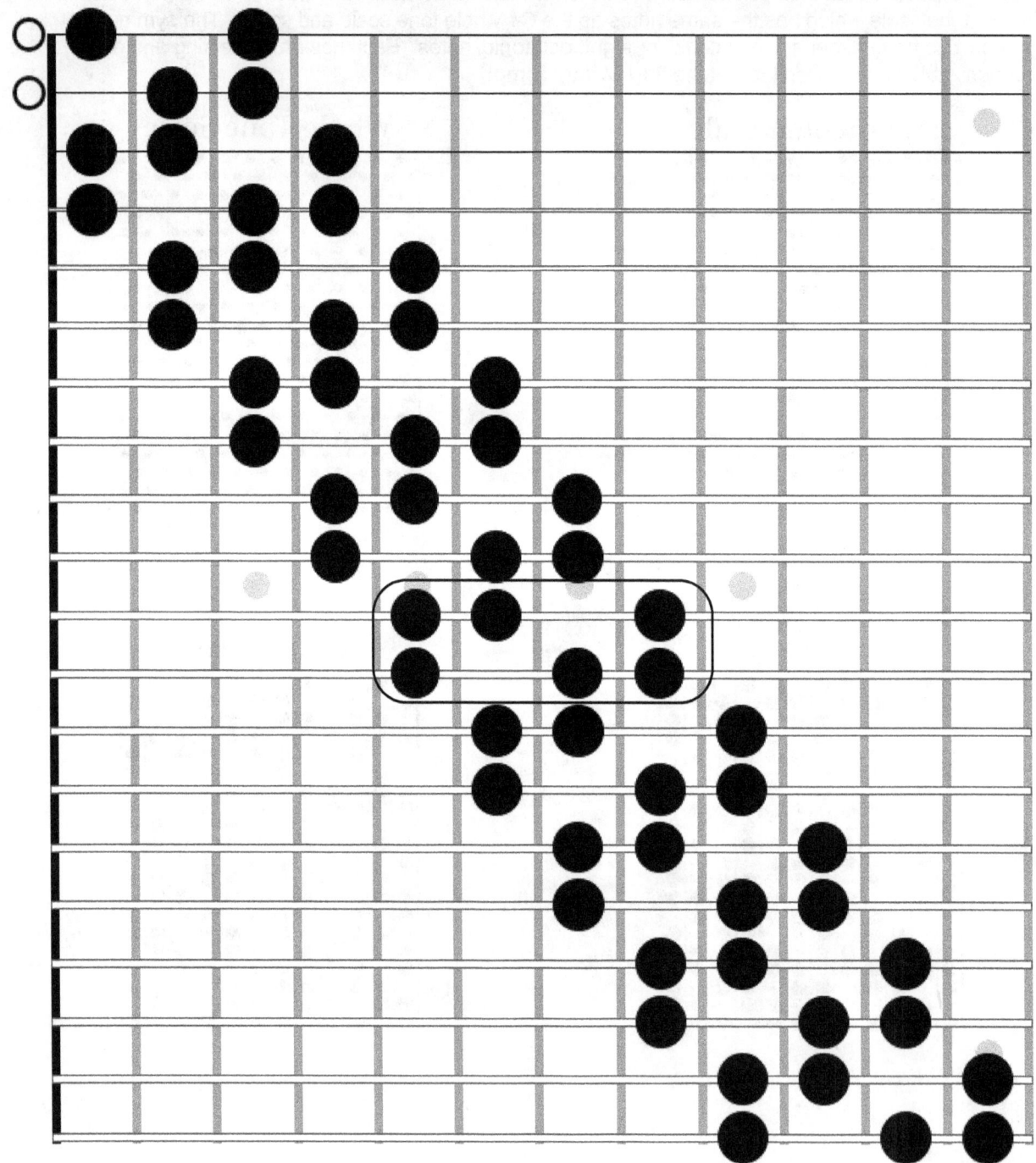

The Whole-1/2 Diminished Scale can be learned quickly because it simply rolls a **134** and a **Small One** dropping back one fret as you repeat the group. Its symmetry creates all kinds of repeating patterns which your brain will uncover as you study the fretboard. Look for these micro structures in ex. 4.

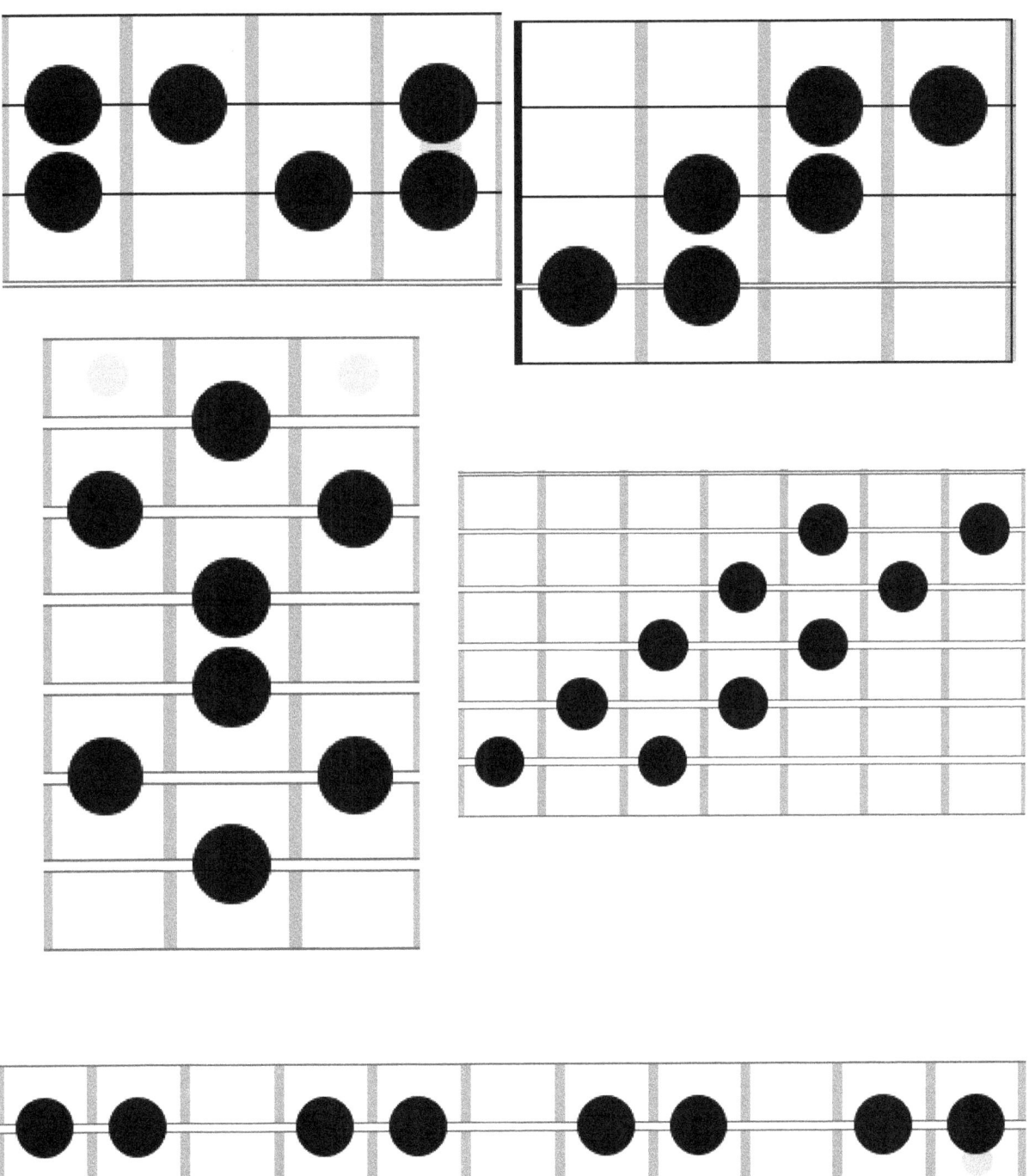

1/2-Whole Diminished

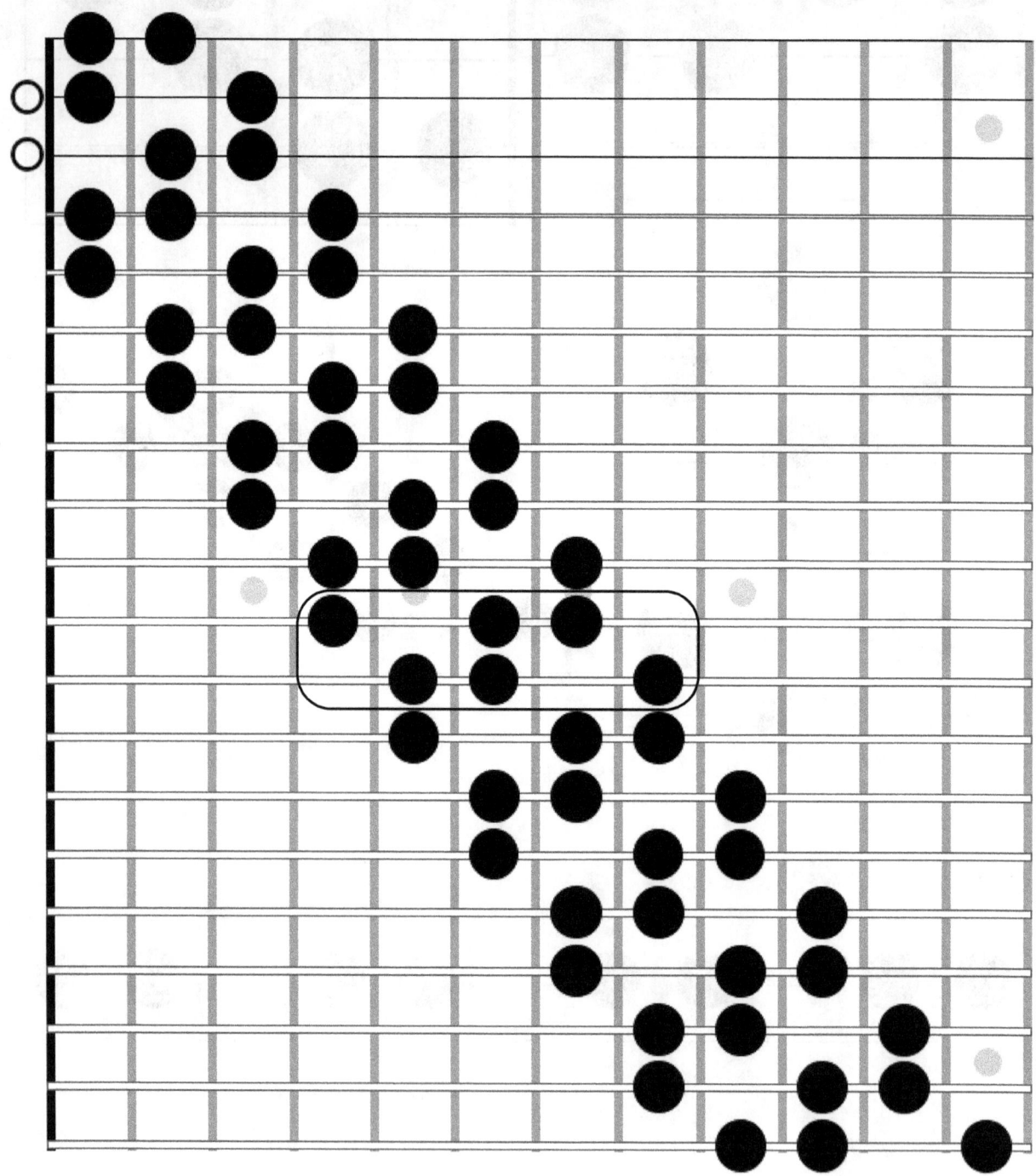

The 1/2-Whole Diminished Scale has the same properties as it's sister scale the Whole-1/2 Diminished. The same patterns can be found but it is basically viewed as beginning with the half step. Check out ex. 4 and you may initially have trouble distinguishing the two diminished scales from one another but look closer and you'll see they are slightly different. Here's a couple more micro structures that can be found within these scales. Yes there's more than I show here.

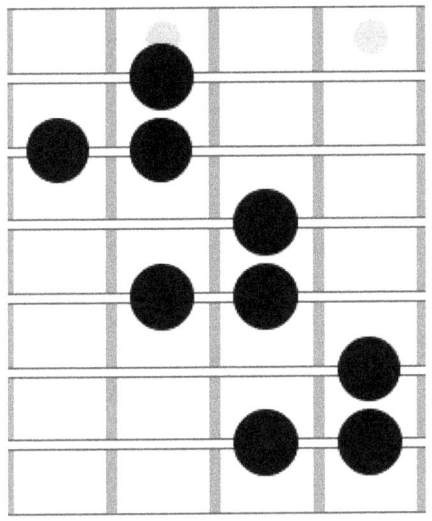

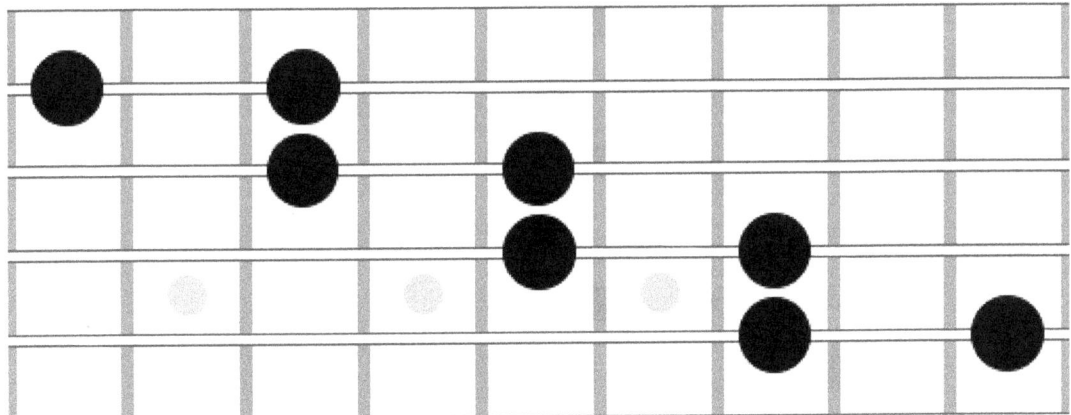

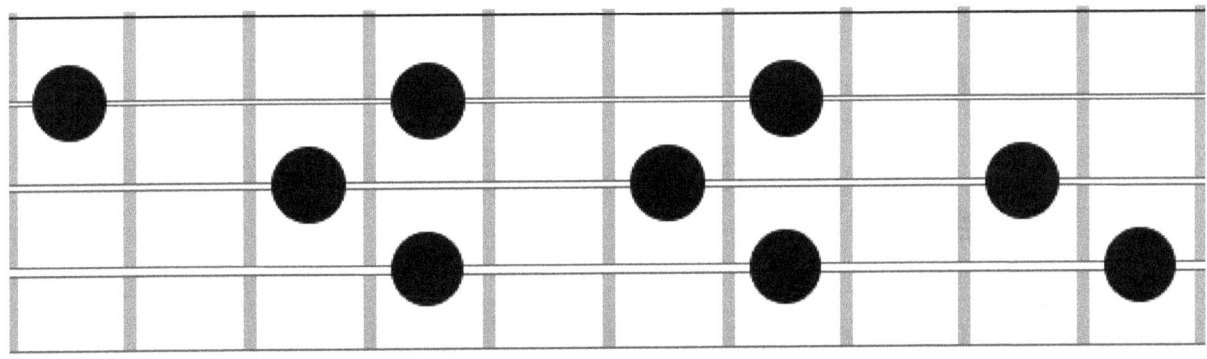

Whole Tone Scale

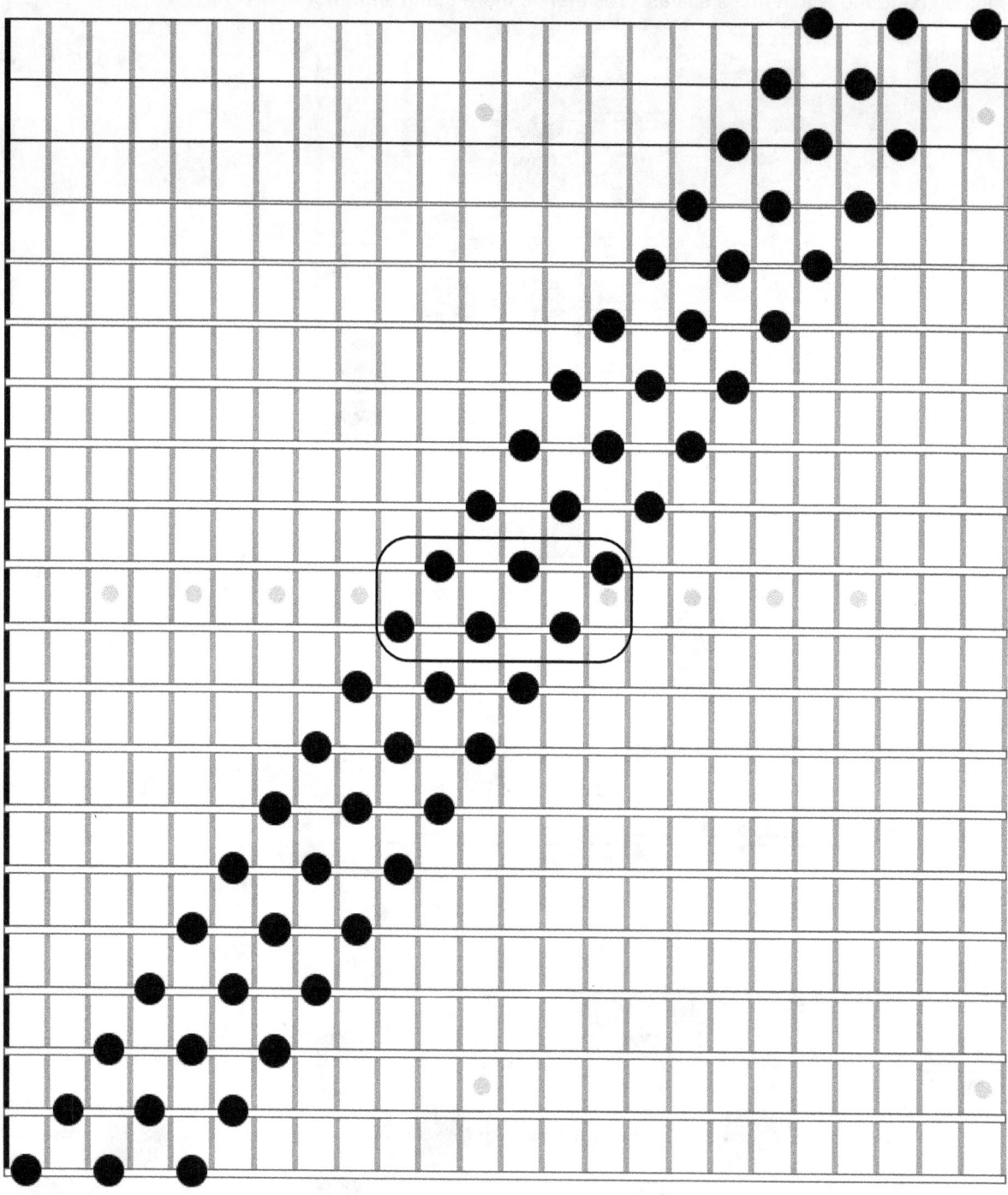

It doesn't get much easier than the Whole Tone Scale. Diagonal **Big Ones** and diamond whole steps as far as the eye can see! Study its full diagram in ex. 4.

Notes and Ideas

<u>Symmetrical scales have an interesting sound. How can I work them into my own music?</u>

Augmented Scale

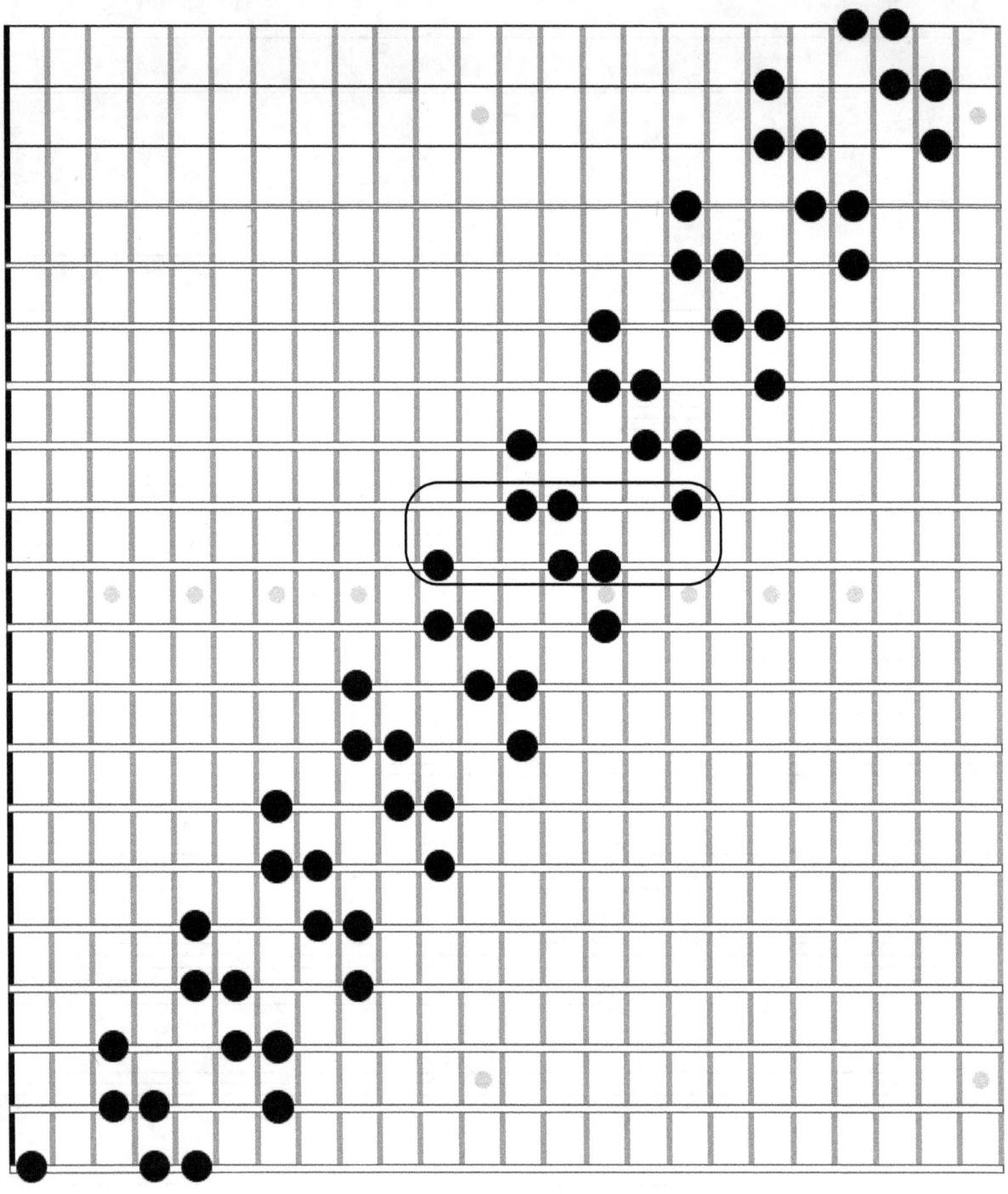

This scale can be viewed as a **1-2** jumping over a fret to a **2-1**. It has some interesting micro structures. See if you can find these patterns. These are just a few, your brain may see more.

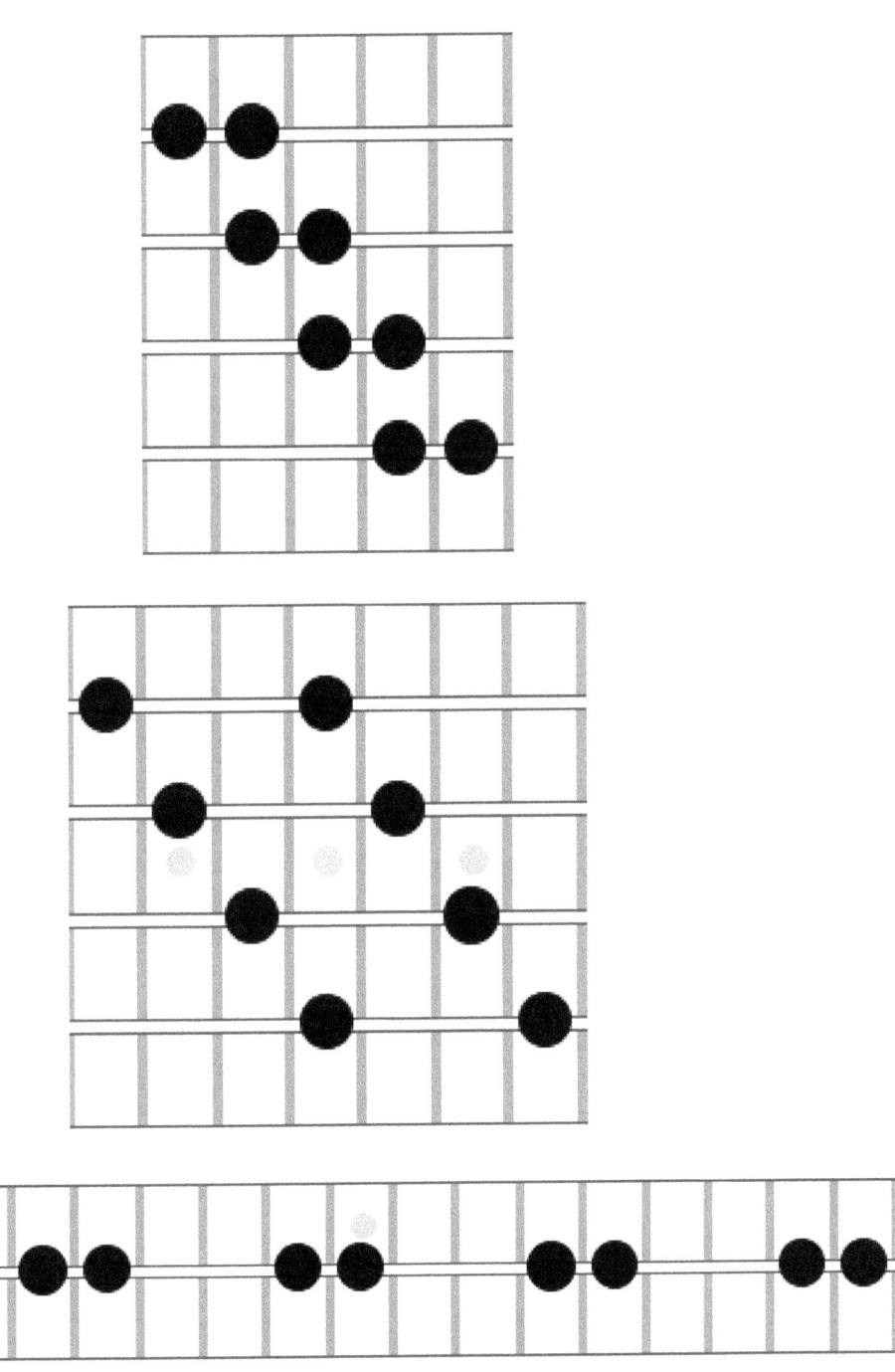

More on Visual Indicators

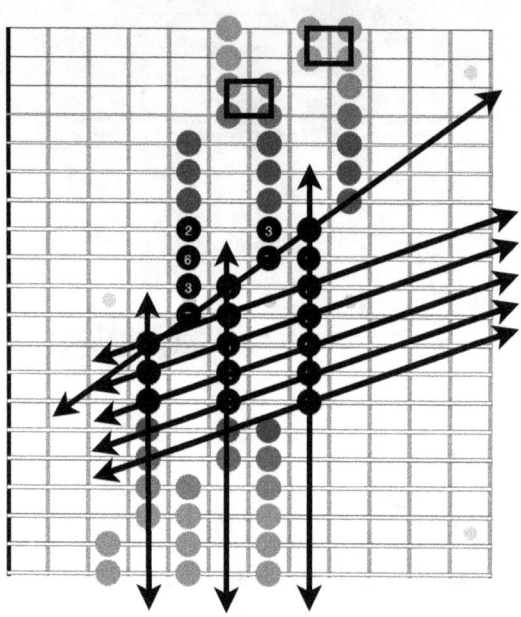

What do you know about the Major Scale from the theory books?

Whole Whole Half, Whole Whole Whole Half. See it?

Major Minor Minor, Major Major Minor, Half Diminished. It's there.

Maybe another way of looking at it will help. How about...

I ii iii IV V vi viib5

or

I IV V and ii iii vi plus a half diminished

or

vii iii vi / -ii- \ V I IV

Confused?

How about...

Stacked 5ths Mr. Russell?

Don't worry, I haven't totally lost it and you're not totally lost. I'm just saying that looking at things from a different angle will help. The theory books tell us that chords built from degrees I, IV, and V of the Major Scale are major. See the Big Ones? The ii, iii, vi, and vii degrees are minor. What do they have in common? Can you find the tritone in the V chord or the b5 in the vii chord or Locrian mode? Did you know that the Major Scale is basically three pentatonics added together? It's all there. Study it, go a little 'John Nash' on it. Just a little though.

Remember the movie, *The Matrix*?

Neo: Is that...

Cypher: The Matrix? Yeah.

Neo: Do you always look at it encoded?

Cypher: Well you have to. The image translators work for the construct program. But there's way too much information to decode the Matrix. **You get used to it. I...I don't even see the code. All I see is blonde, brunette, red-head.** Hey, you uh... want a drink?

By now you may feel like you need a drink but if you study the 50 String Guitar you may stop seeing the code. All you'll see is major, minor, diminished, augmented....

Major Triad
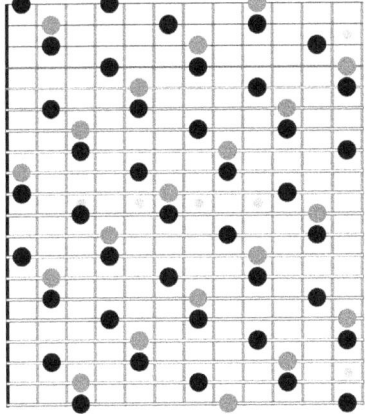

Minor Triad
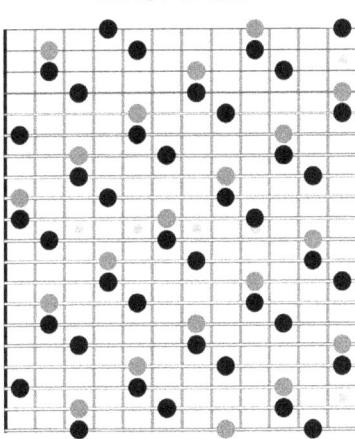

Diminished Triad
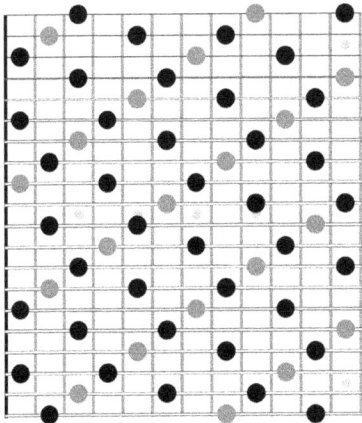

Augmented Triad
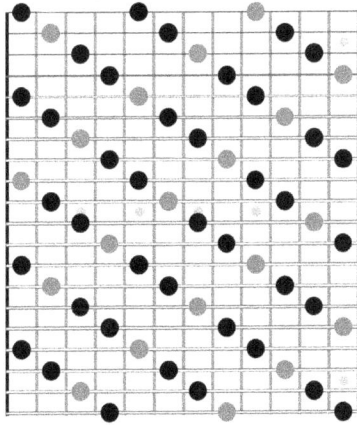

Mentally superimpose the triads on the previous page onto these scale charts. What do you see in the matrix?

Major Scale

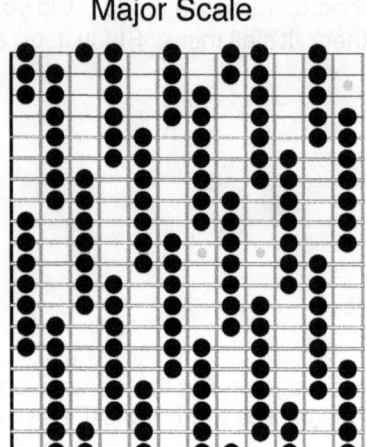

Harmonic Minor

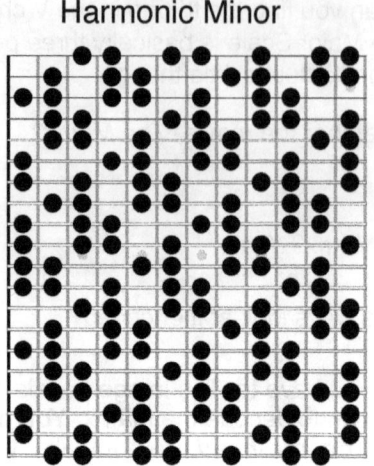

Melodic Minor

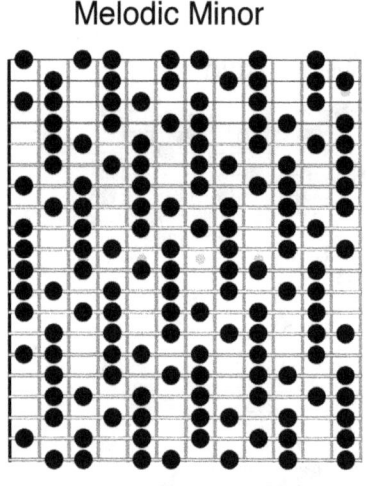

Harmonic Major

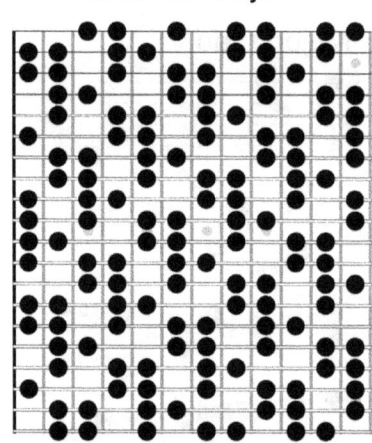

Whole Tone Scale

Diminished

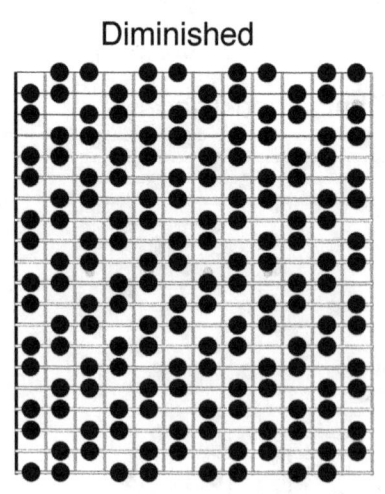

Here's a few examples to examine involving the Major Scale. If we know it well, we can know the others more easily.

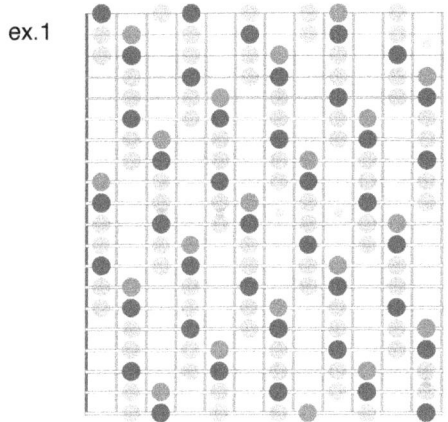
ex.1

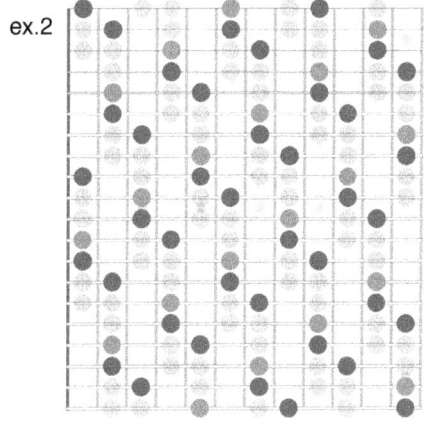
ex.2

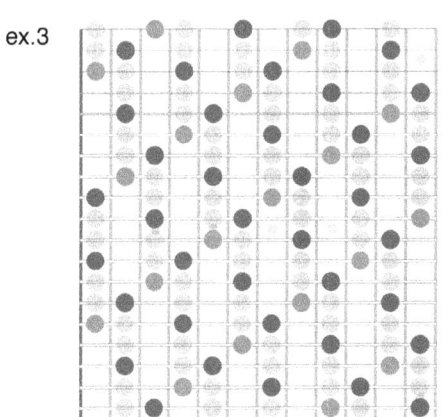
ex.3

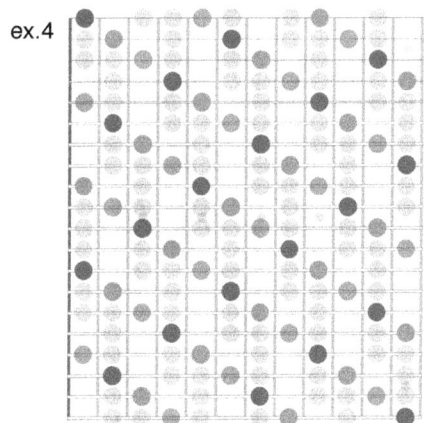
ex.4

In example 1 above we have a major triad superimposed on the major scale. Example 2 has a minor triad superimposed on the major scale. In example 3 we have a diminished triad superimposed on the major scale. Example 4 has a augmented triad superimposed on the major scale which does not work. A quick glance at the major scale and you'll see that there is no augmented triad in it. So what is all this?

The Modal Number

4152637415263741526374152637415263741526374152637....

All that we musicians do can be described using math. Given to us by the primes in the creation and expansion of the 1, each note is a invitation to return to the 1 and a pathway there.

I suppose it is more than just math. If it sounds mystical, spiritual.....well, to some it is. We want to return to the 1. The 1 wants us to return. The evidence is abundant but for now lets return to the 50 String Guitar!

Using numbers will enhance our knowledge of the scales and one number is prevalent on the 50 String Guitar. 4152637... This number falls down vertically on the matrix of the 50 String Guitar in every 7 note scale. It is half of the great circle of 5ths. It is a numerical representation of the fundamental building blocks of western music and the tonal gravity within. Check it out in the Major Scale below.

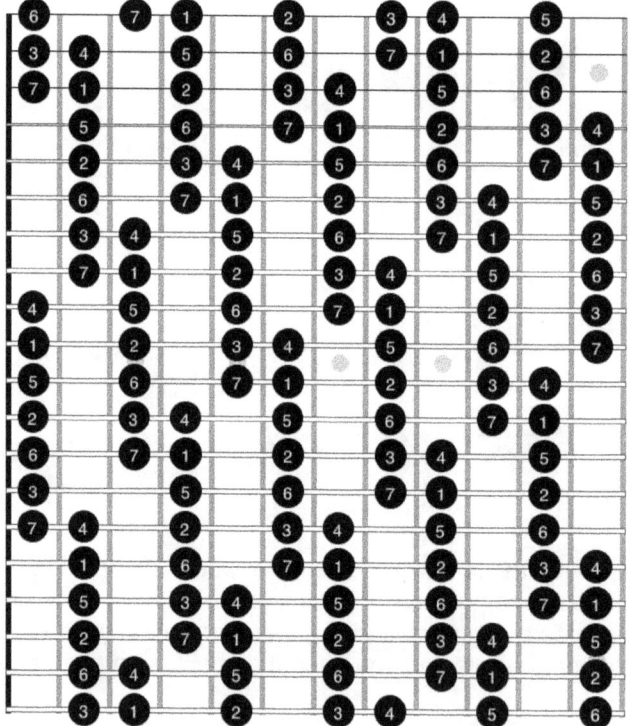

You may find that the Modal Number is most useful when improvising. Knowing this well, you can freely move horizontally on the your guitar and still know what part of the pattern is above or below your current position. It can help when playing over key changes as well. You may find another reason to know the Modal Number.

Try looking at these scales in 5th intervals (or 4ths depending on which direction you're going). Learn the Modal Number. Remember we are still on the 50 String Guitar so the 2nd String Jump rule still applies. Now, all of the information about the Major Scale is contained in the codes below. We just need to decipher them.

Here you see seven different views of the major scale. They could correspond to the seven modes of the scale or we could say that they are just different ways to see the Major Scales' Modal Number. They are all the same thing but which one is easiest on the brain? I believe it is the one in the middle. A perfect stack of perfect 4ths (or 5ths depending on how you look at it). The Modal Number! I will focus on this view of the Code but the others should be studied as they display an interesting properties. One of which is called roto-reflection symmetry described below. Do you hear it? (hint: Major type vs. Minor type)

Roto-reflection

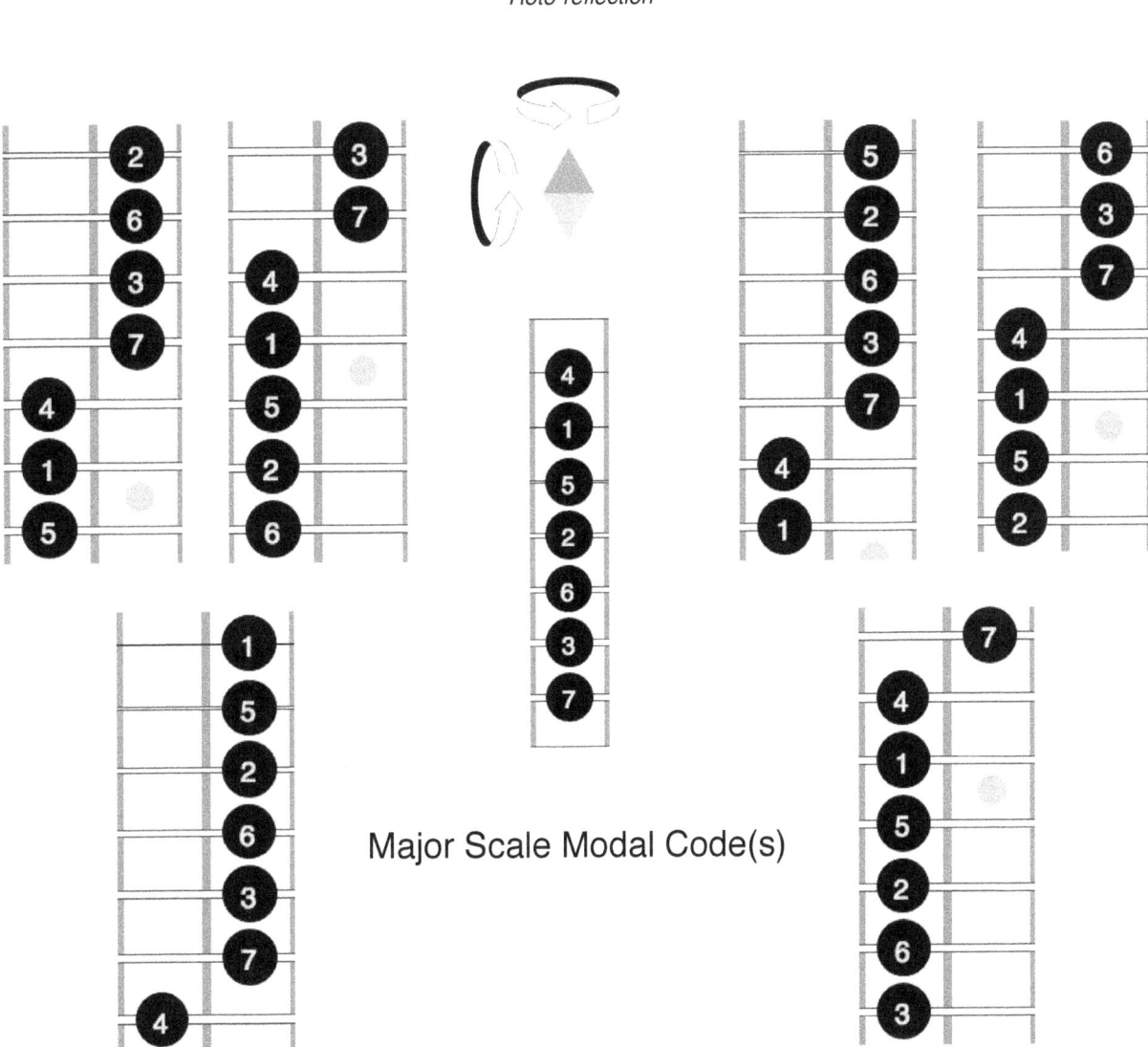

Major Scale Modal Code(s)

The Master Code

Before we look at individual scales again we should take a moment to get to know what I call The Master Code. It is the complete stack of 5ths/4ths on the 50 String Guitar. It shows the circle of fifths in linear fashion and as you can see the Major Scale is right in the middle. Alterations all fall above or below the center scale, flats on top and sharps on bottom. No need to memorize this now. Or is there? Just know it is the repeating Modal Number with flats on top and sharps on bottom.

Flat Alterations:
- b5
- b2
- b6
- b3
- b7

Major Scale:
- p4
- 1
- p5
- Δ2
- Δ6
- Δ3
- Δ7

Sharp Alterations:
- #4
- #1
- #5
- #2
- #6

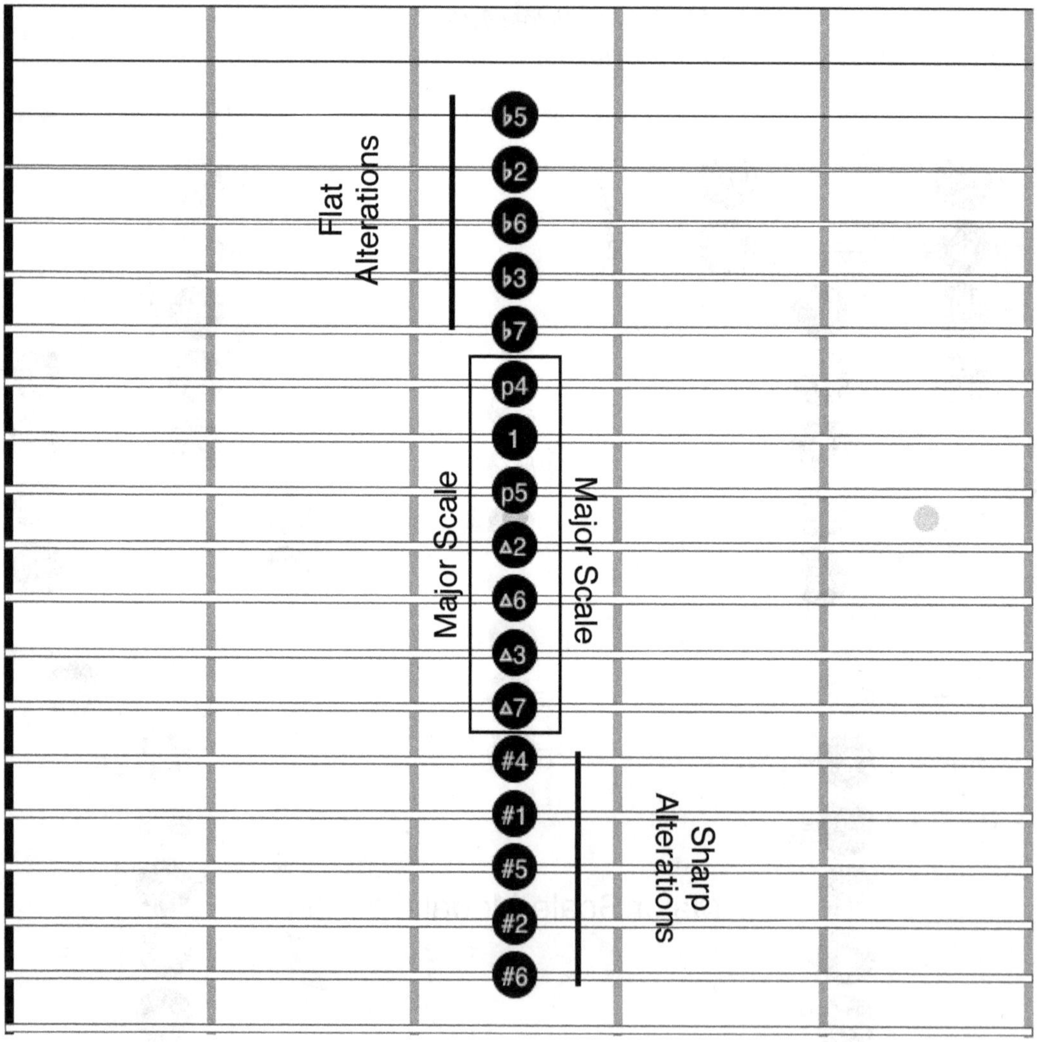

Modal Comparison

(Point of View)

Which mode of the Major Scale is this? 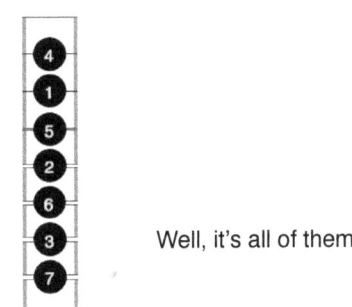 Well, it's all of them.

It just depends on how you look at it, that is to say, where the 1 is.

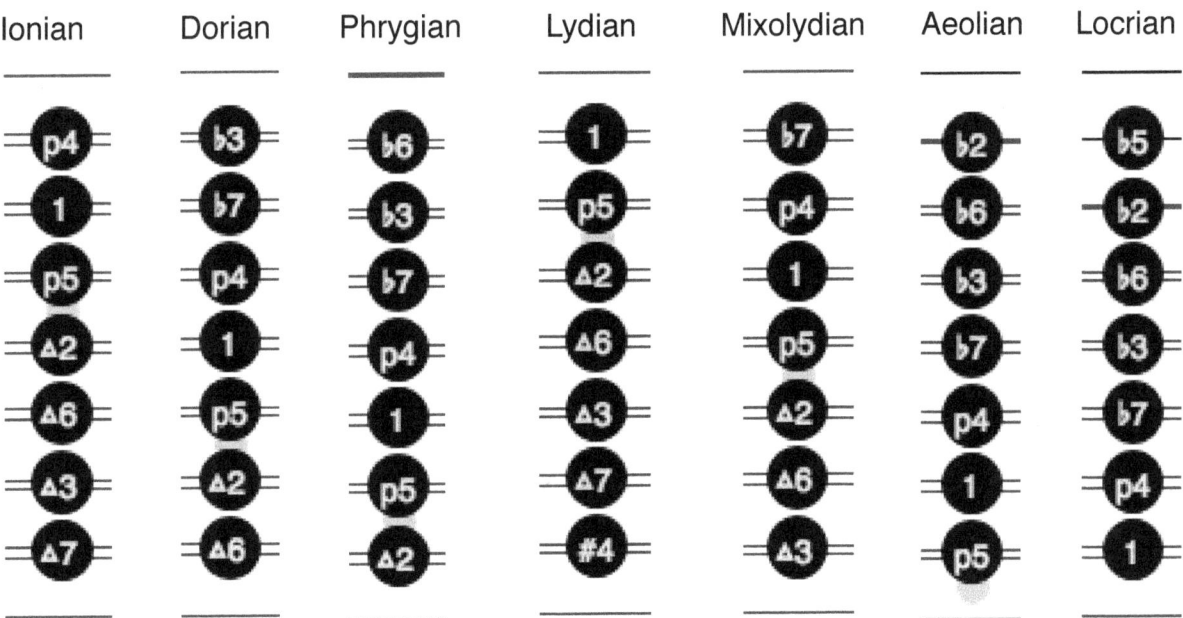

Take Lydian for example. We have put the 1 in the place of the perfect 4th of the major scale. This reveals the construction of the Lydian Scale. It shows that Lydian has all of the same intervals as the Major Scale (Ionian) 1, p5, Δ2, Δ6, Δ3 and Δ7 except one change, the #4. You can imagine that the p4 dropped down into the sharp alteration territory in the Master Code. Another way of visualization is to imagine that the rectangle around the Major Scale in the Master Code above has moved down encasing the #4 and no longer containing the p4.

Move the perfect Δ7 into flat alteration territory and you get Mixolydian. Mixolydian has the same construction as the Major Scale but with a flatted 7th degree. Similarly you can use the Master Code or the Modal Number to learn the construction of all modes when compared to the Major Scale. Remember if we know the Major Scale inside and out we can know all other scale more easily. You can reveal the formulas for any mode of any scale! Can you find other implications?

Major Scale Modal Code

All intervals "normal"

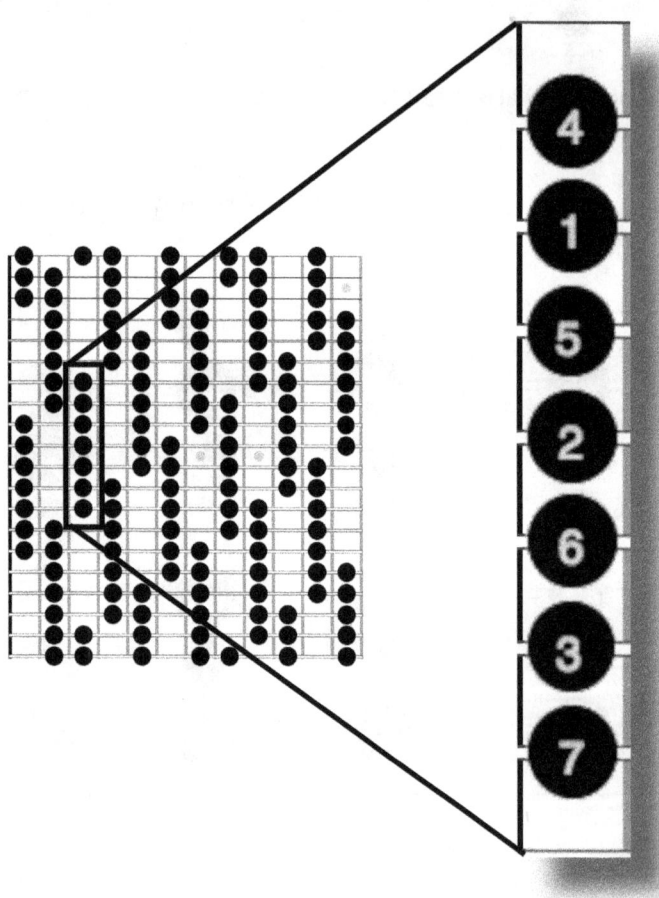

Melodic Minor Modal Code

Compared to the Major Scale the 3rd degree has been moved into the flat territory of the Master Code.

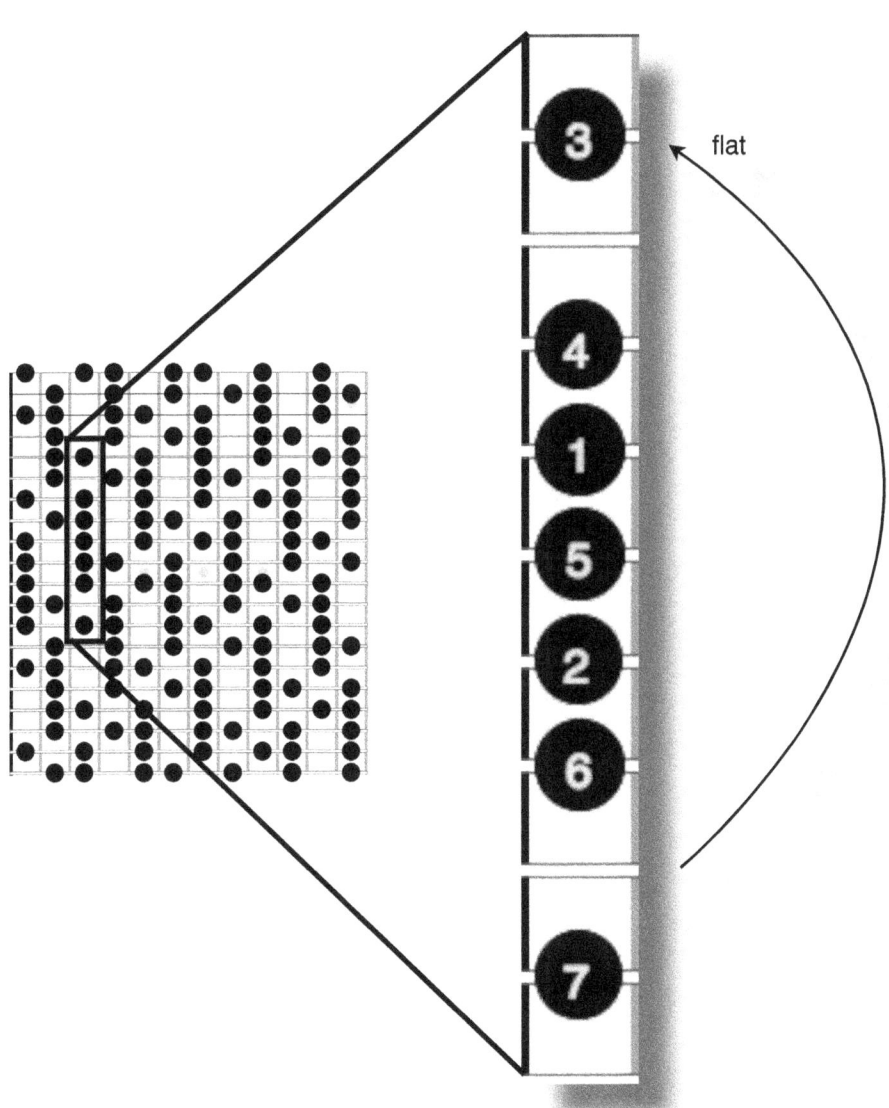

Harmonic Minor Modal Code

Compared to Major, Harmonic Minor has a flatten 3rd and 6th degree. It is only one notes difference from Melodic Minor.

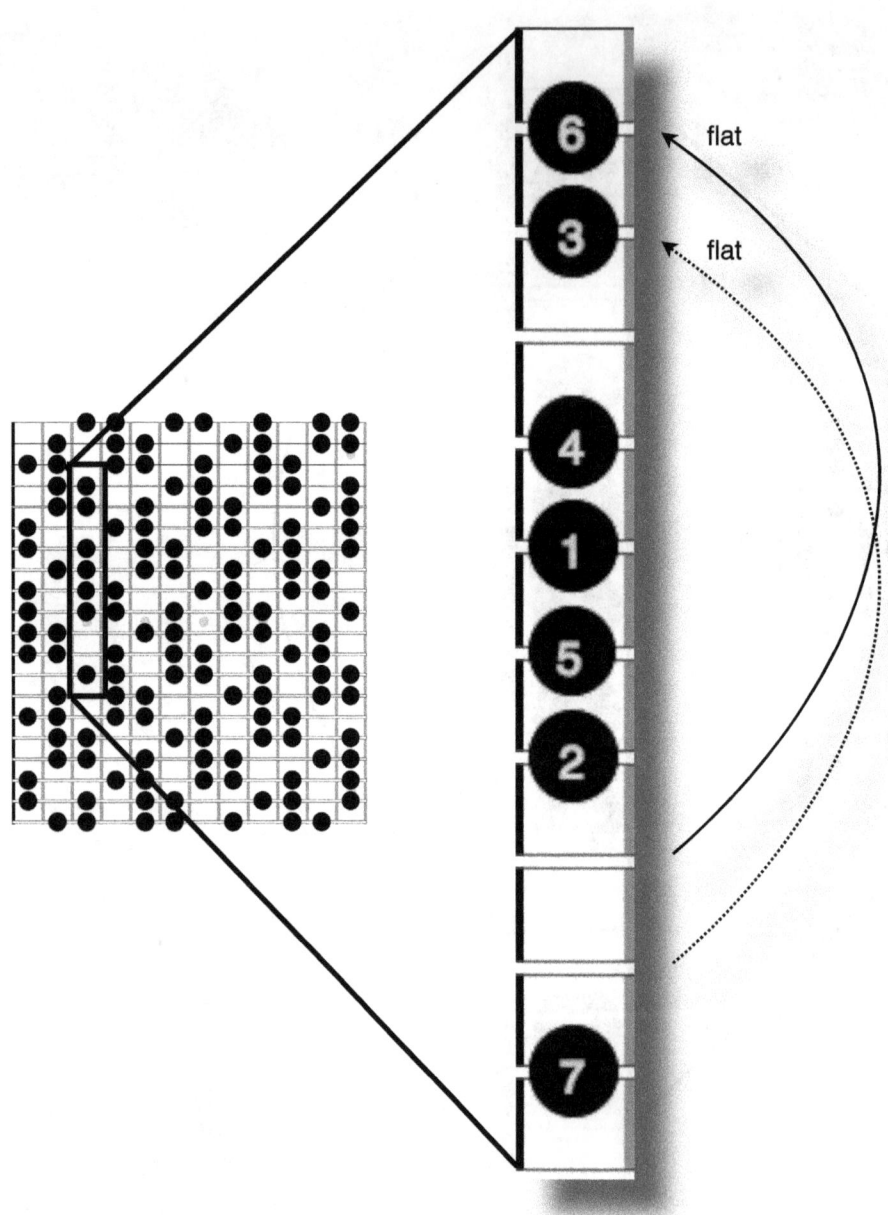

Harmonic Major Modal Code

Harmonic Major is just like the major scale except the flatten 6th degree. It has a reflective symmetry with Harmonic Minor.

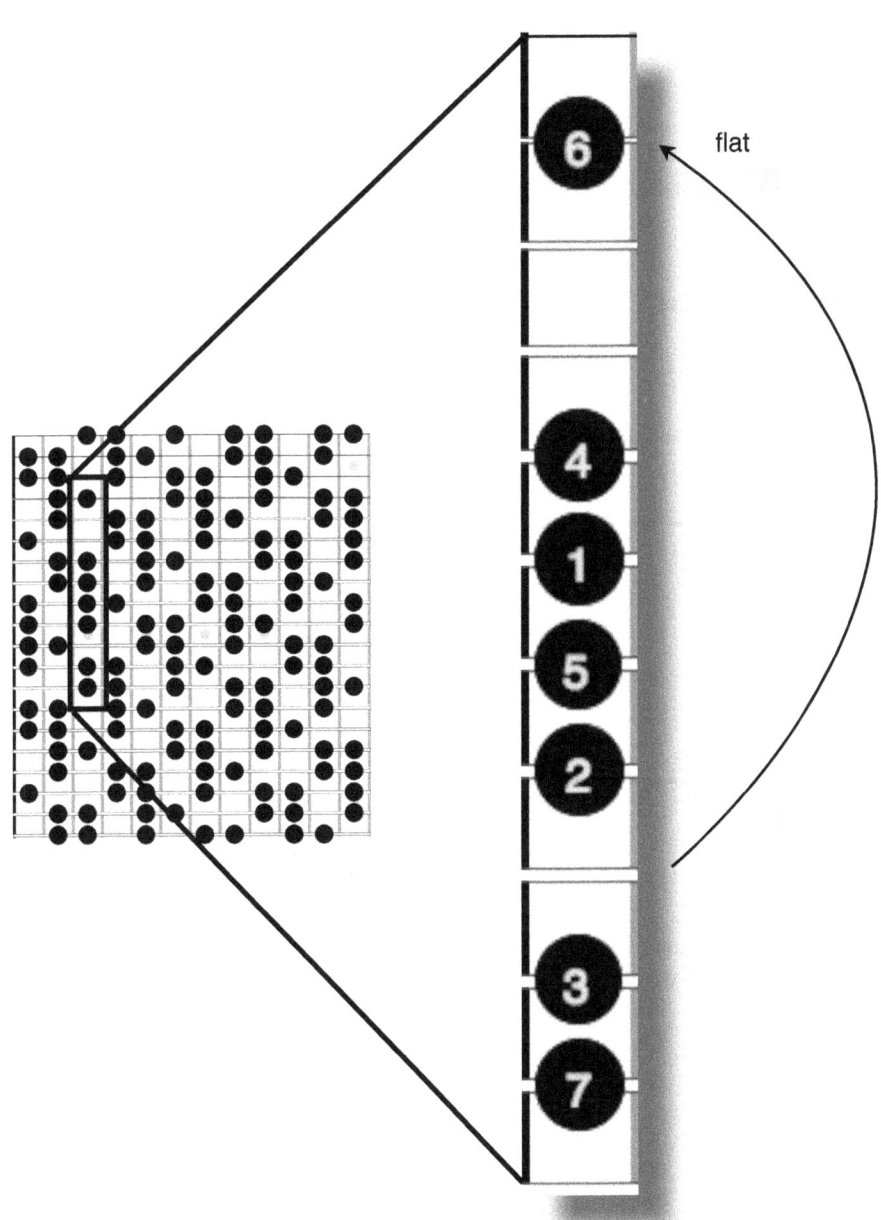

Modal Matrices

Earlier we looked at different types of triads (chords) on the 50 String Guitar. We superimposed them over the Major Scale and saw that some were in the scale and some were not. In this next section we look into each scales Matrix and view its inner structures. I show the standard triads and 7th chords that can be built with each scale. To me the best parts of learning and using these scales is improvising with them over a beautiful harmony. Although this book does not focus on chords one must learn the harmonies within each scale to fully utilize them. Here I show triads and 7th chords but there are many more combinations such as clusters, sus4s, 6 chords, 9ths, 11ths, 13ths, etc... You do the math. No really, DO THE MATH.

Using the Master Code and the principles discussed in the Modal Comparison chapter you should be able to find the chord formula for any chord shown on the Matrices below. Here's an example.

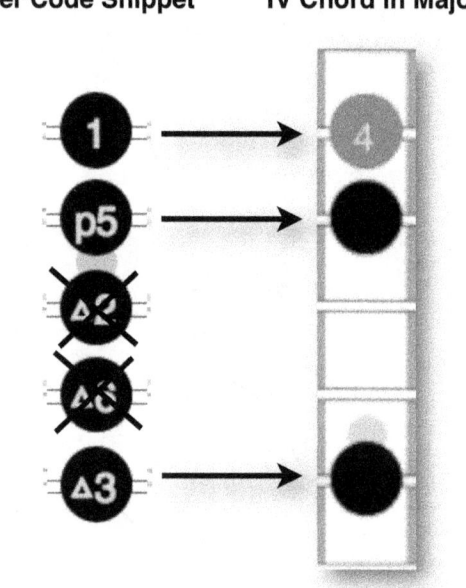

One can see that the major IV chord in the Major Scale is built with a 1 (root), perfect 5th, and a major 3rd. Apply the Master Code to all the chords below to learn their structure and formula.

Major Matrix

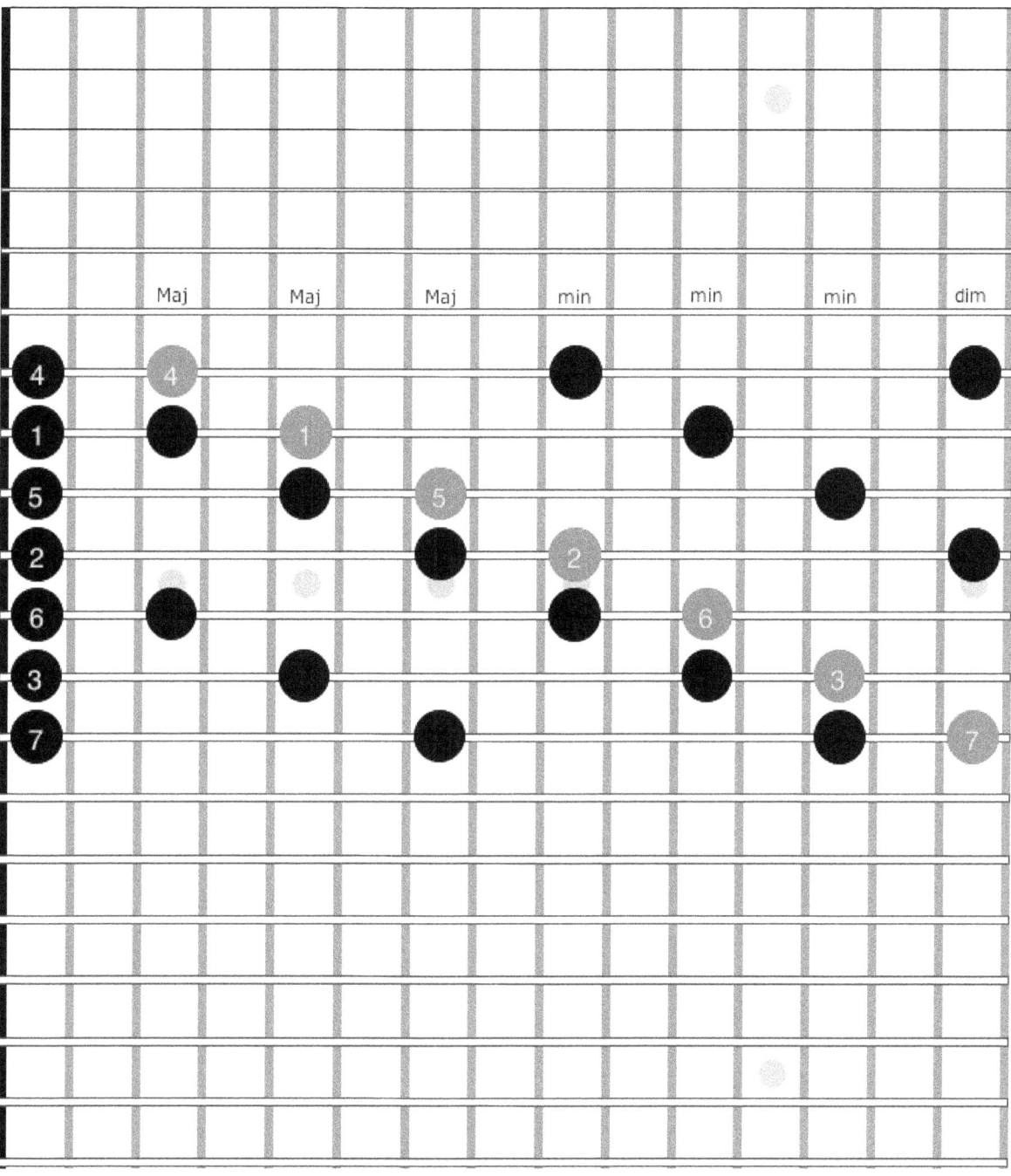

Major Matrix 7ths

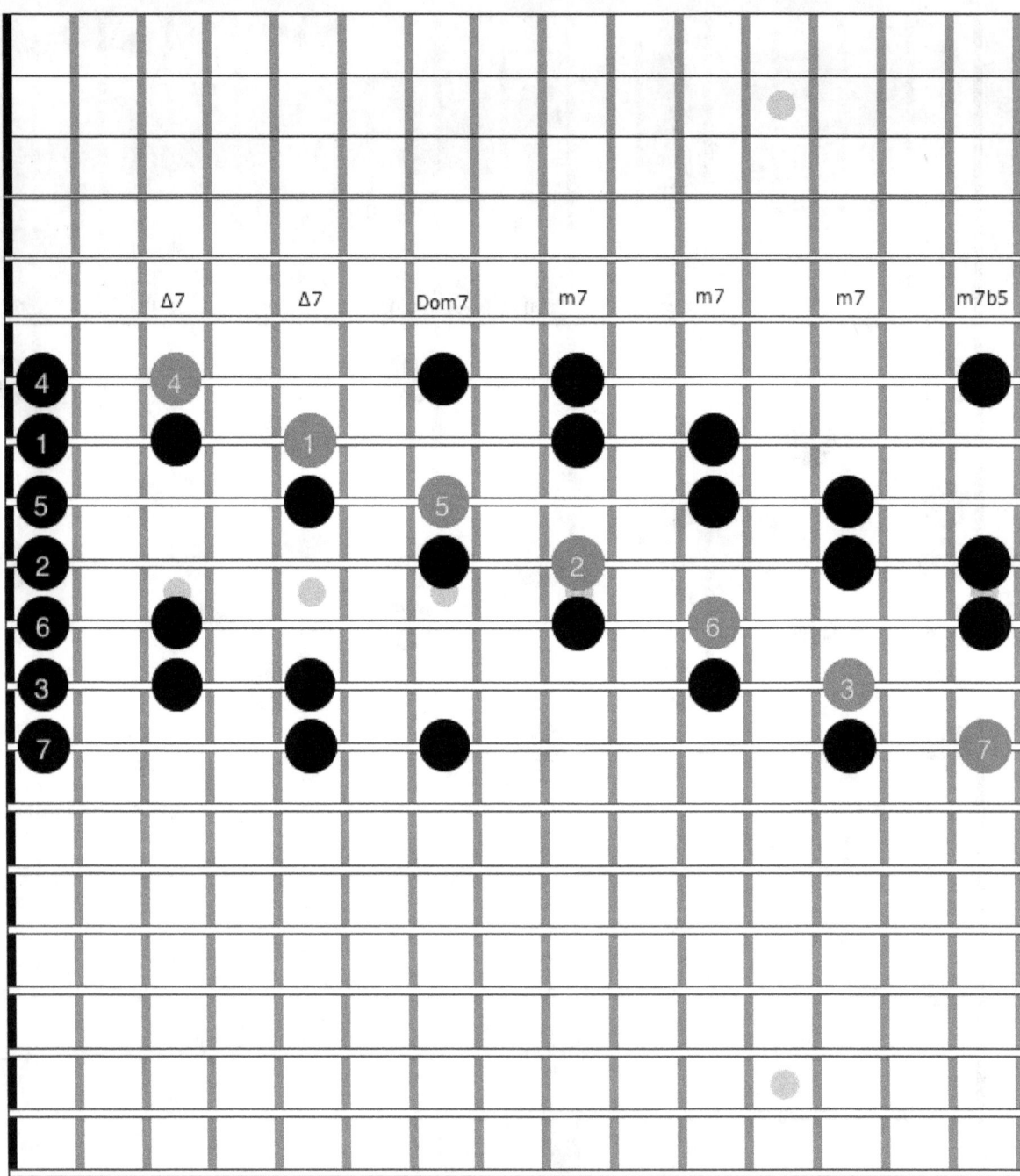

Learn the Major Scale *thoroughly* and you should be able to identify each of the triads and chords that are not labeled in the following pages.

Melodic Minor Matrix

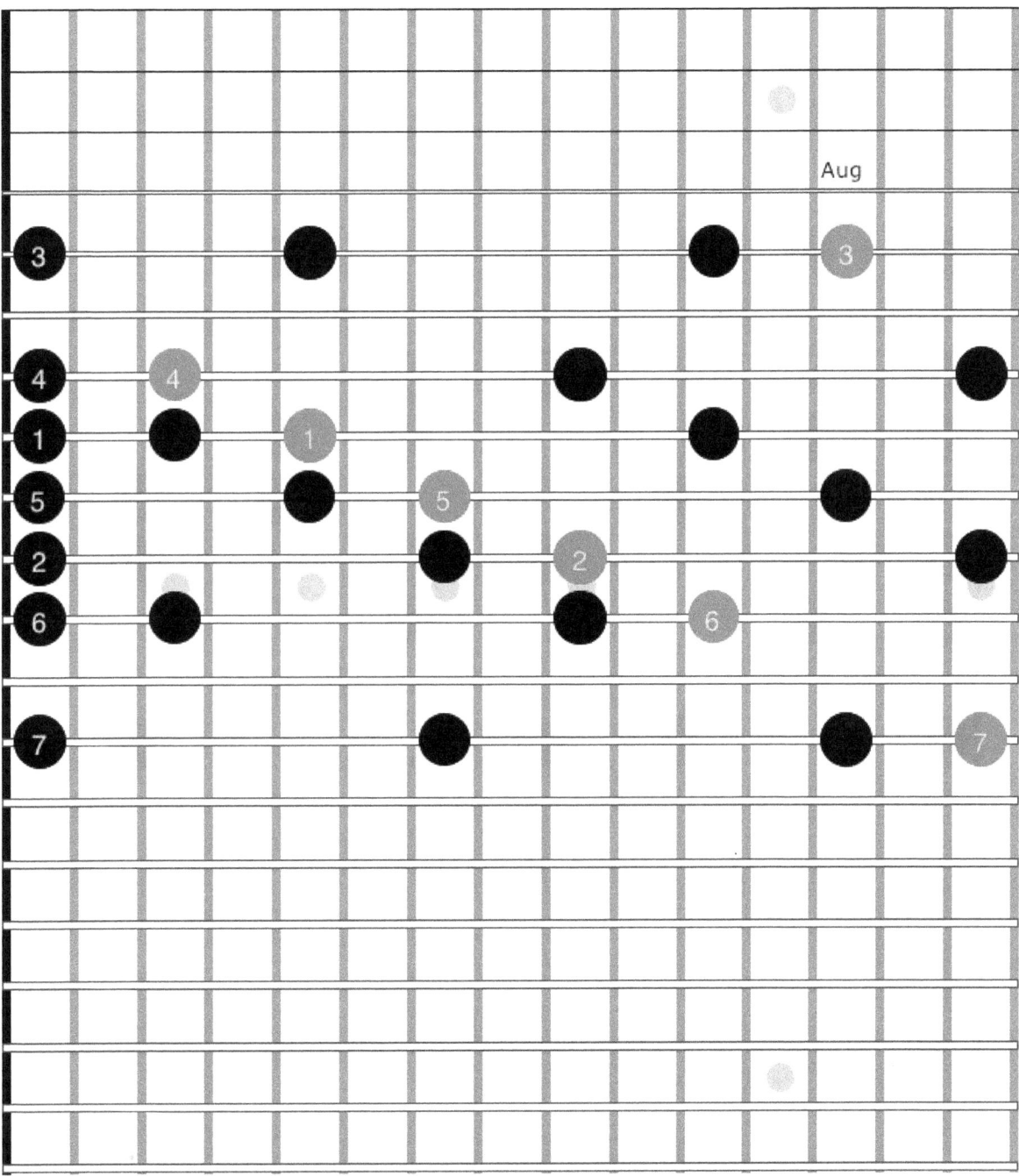

A new Augmented triad is found in the Melodic Minor Scale. You will see it again.

Melodic Minor Matrix 7ths

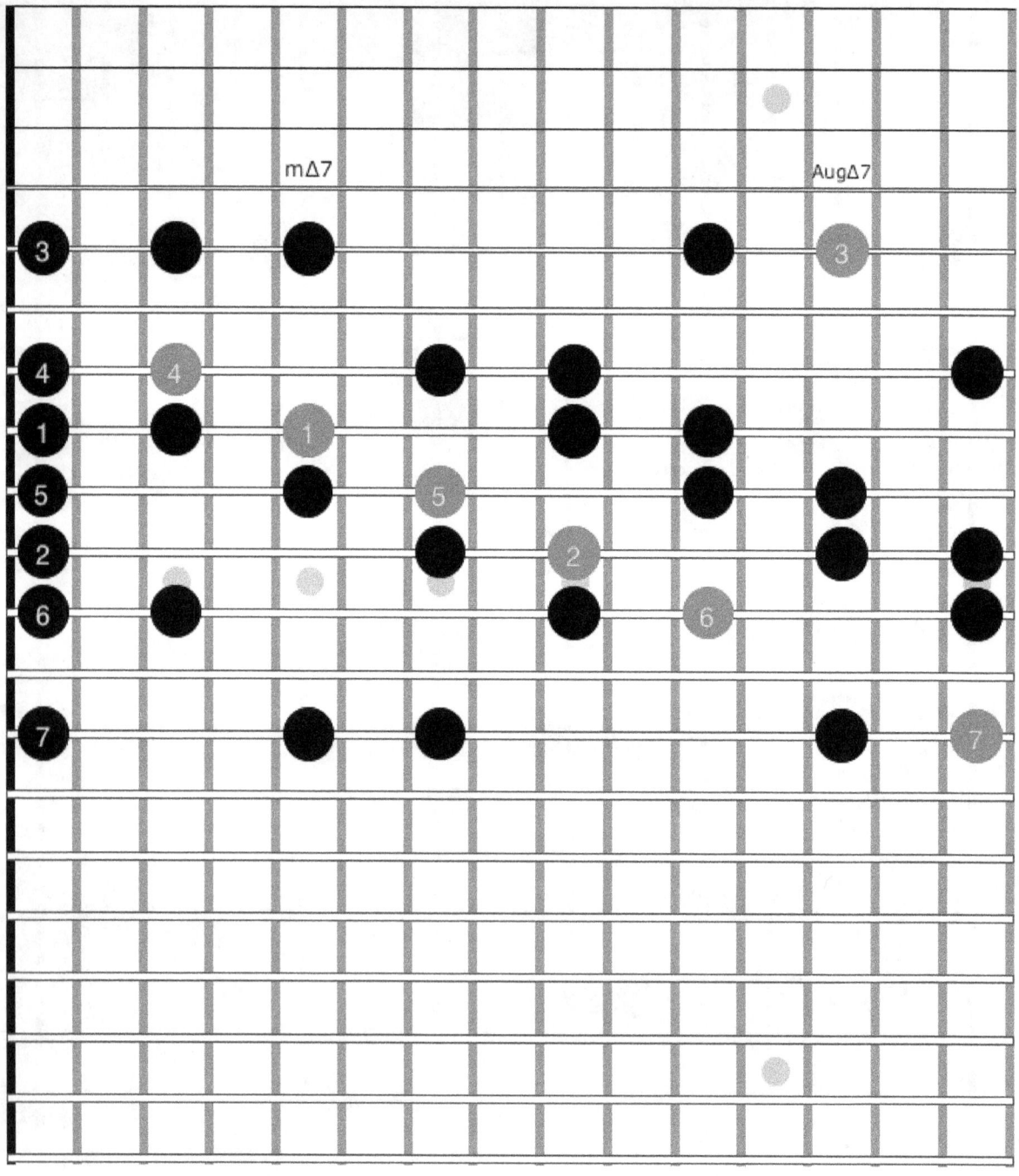

We see a minor major 7th chord and an augmented major 7th chord here in Melodic Minor.

Harmonic Minor Matrix

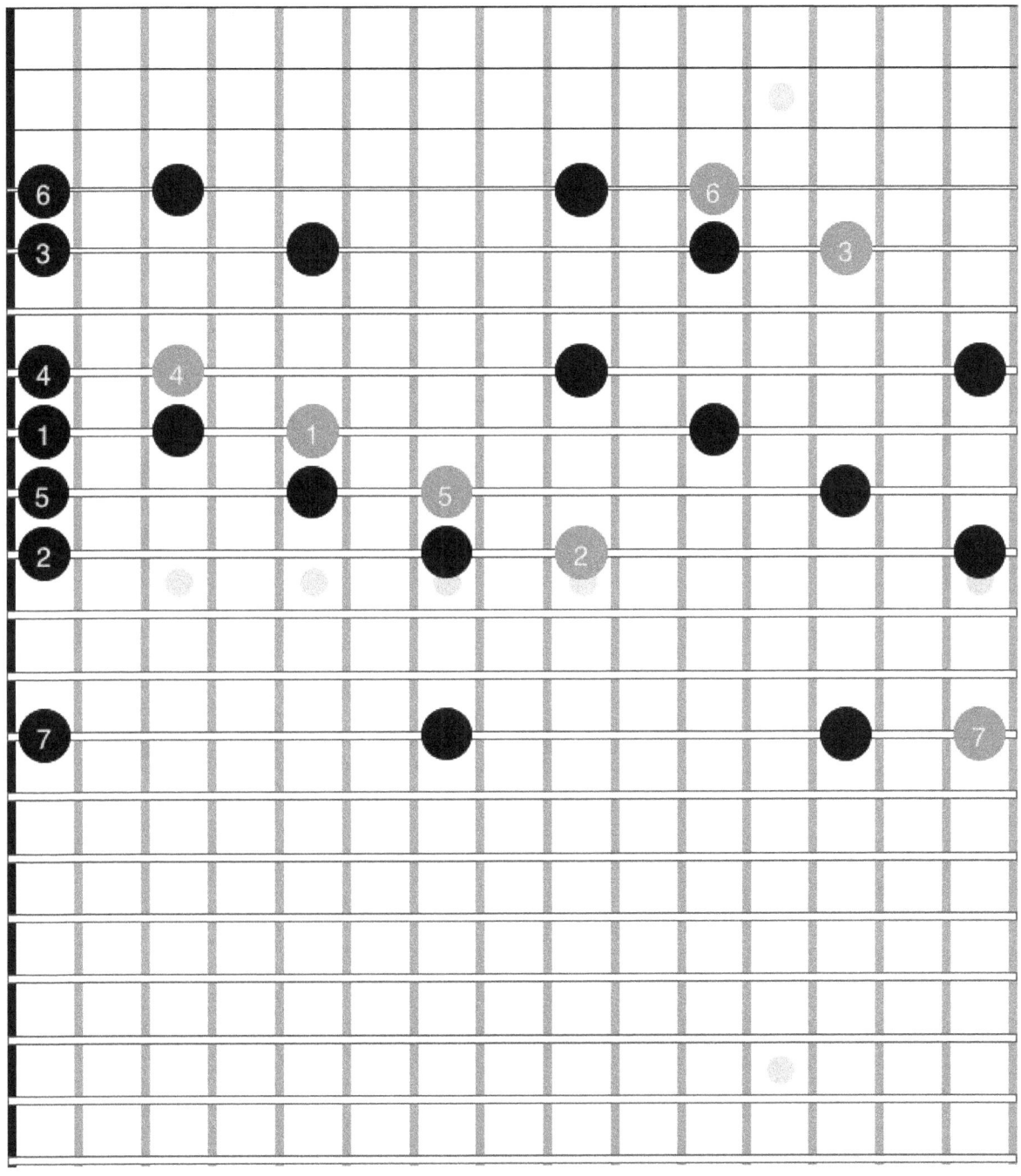

Harmonic Minor Matrix 7ths

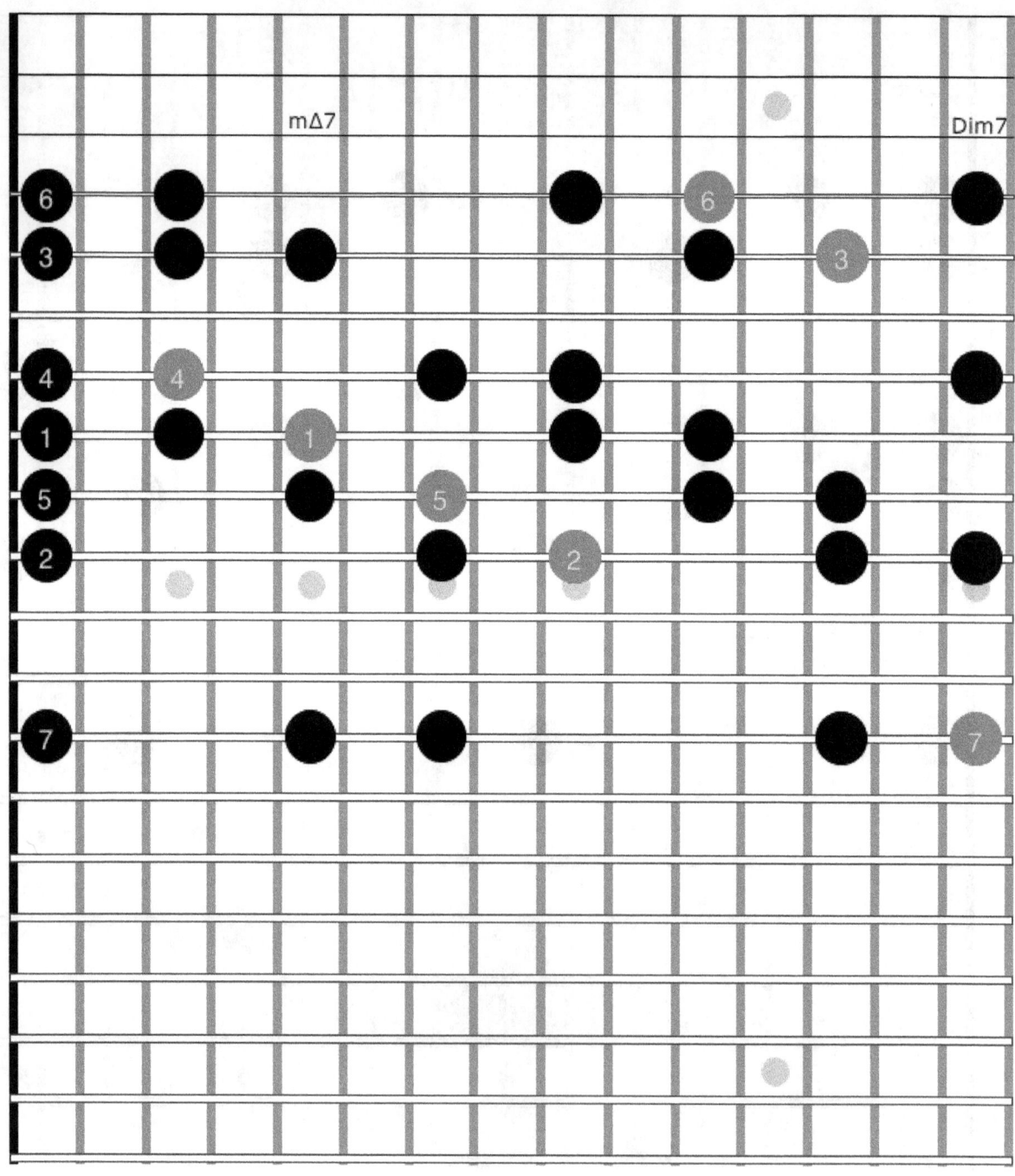

Harmonic Major Matrix

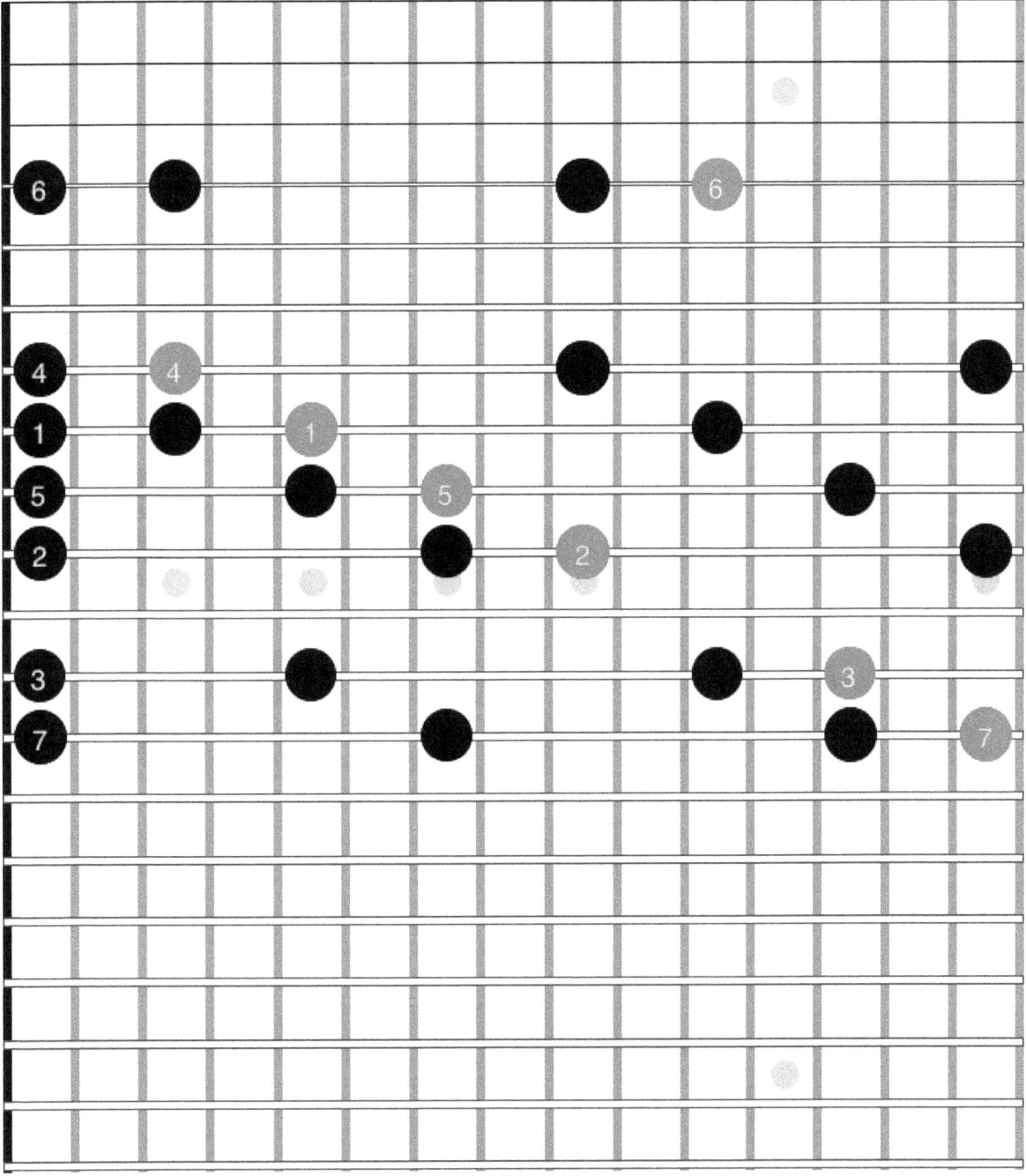

Harmonic Major Matrix 7ths

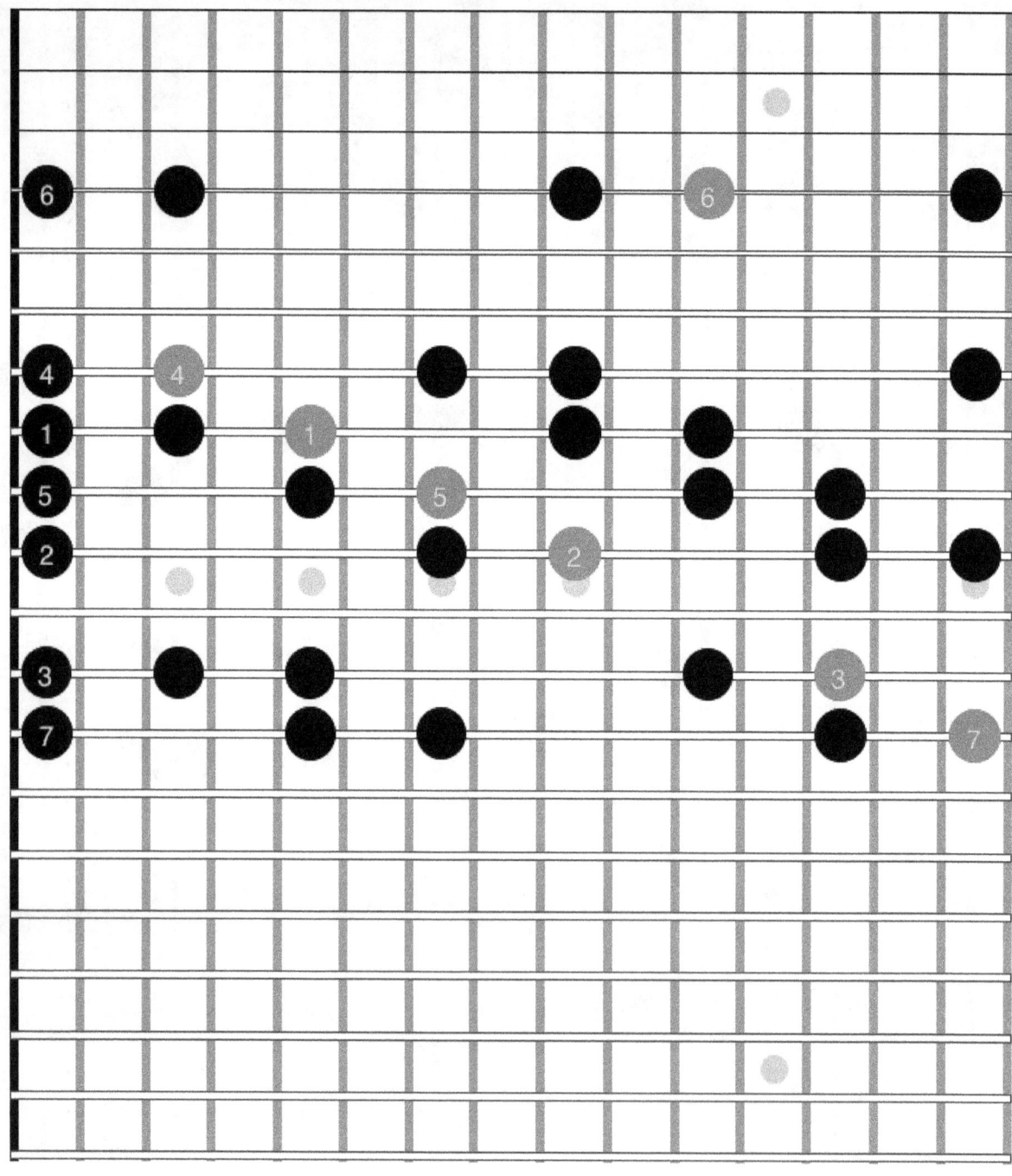

If you've studied the Major, Melodic, and Harmonic Minor scales you should be able to identify all of the chords in Harmonic Major. A good exercise would be to label all of the unlabeled chords above. Write their formulas below each one in numerical order. For example, the IV chord in Harmonic Major is mΔ7 chord with the formula 1, b3, p5, and Δ7. **Then play them!** Use the Interval Study/Reference in the appendix to help build them on your guitar.

Moving Beyond

I have shown that by knowing a few simple basic shapes and how they revolve on the 50 String Guitar we can more easily learn the most common and even the most advanced scales on the standard guitar. Using the Major Scale as our archetypal scale, just as the major chord is the archetypal chord, one can more easily learn all other scales. We have seen that it is easier to know Melodic Minor as Ionian b3 and Harmonic Minor as Aeolian #7 and we have renamed the modes accordingly.

We have delved further into the structures that are easily visualized on the 50 Stringed Guitar but not so on the 6 string. We studied the Modal Number and Master Code to reveal the formulas for any scale and chord. This information has been around for hundreds of years but we are looking at it in a new way, one designed for guitarists, both teachers and students. Share it with your student and teacher!

Next we will take a sneak peak beyond the common scales. Some may call them more "exotic" scales but by now we know that they are just more mathematical possibilities of the 12 tones we have at our disposal on the guitar. This is not to diminish them in any way. These 12 tones are responsible for vast variety and beauty. And fun! Let's learn more.

More "Exotic" Scales

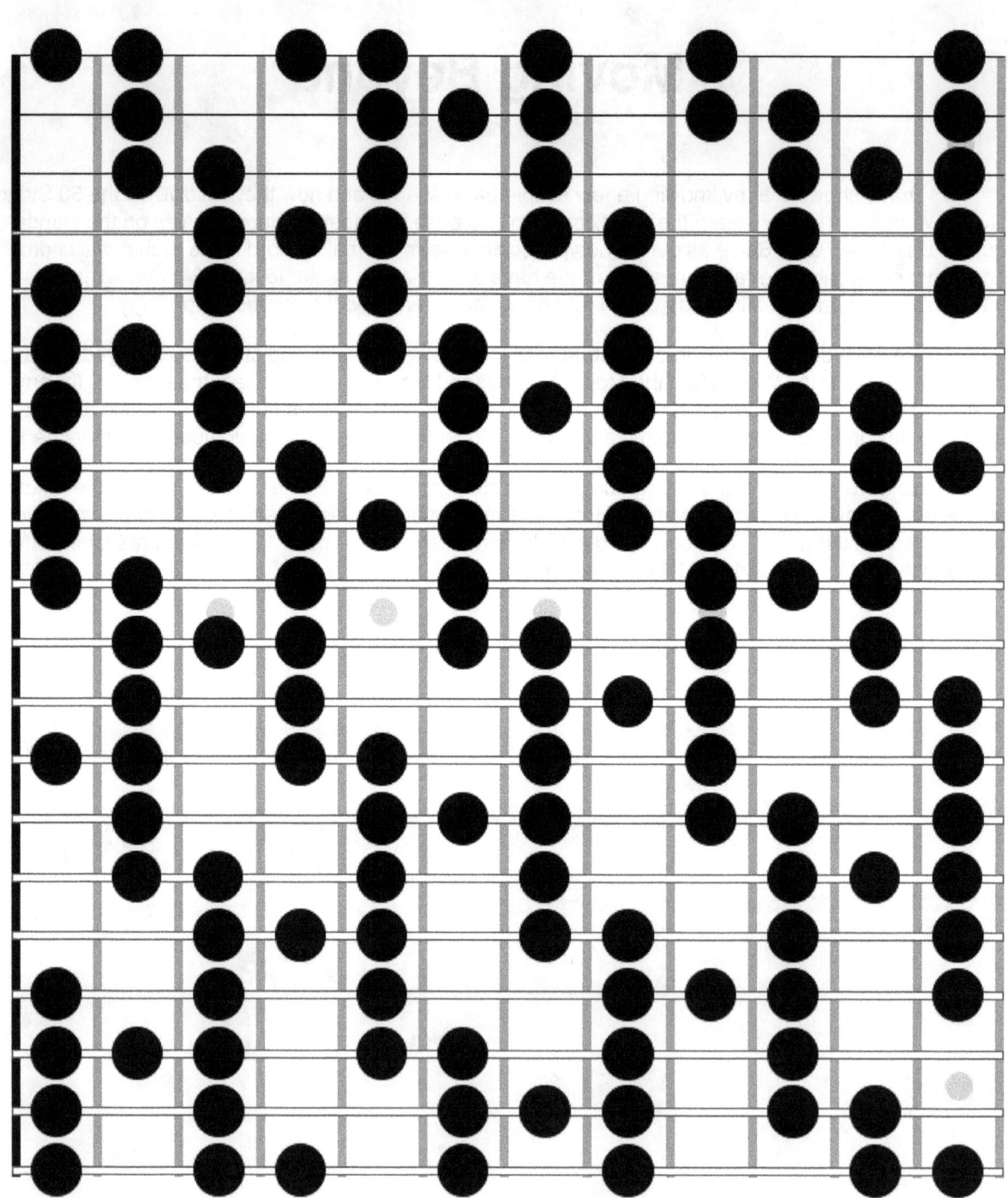

What's the name of this scale? I doesn't matter! (After all that complaining about names earlier and I say, "It doesn't matter!") At a glance we can see it contains 2 pentatonics on the 1st and 4th degrees, an augmented triad, and a diminished triad. Its formula is 1 #1/b2 2 3 4 5 6. Some of the chords that can be built from this scale are I, bIIaugΔ7, ii7, IIIaug7, IVΔ7, Vaug, and iv7. Yes, there are more.

As an exercise analyze the modes of this scale using the Master Code, identify the basic shapes and their revolving pattern, look for microstructures and visual indicators, and compare it to the Major Scale.

Have your teacher or student play a progression with these chords while the other plays the scale over top. This is a great way to really get to know the sound of the scale. After all, it's about sharing beauty (and other colors) with others.

There are many more scales available for exploration. Use the Blanks for Printing and Study in the appendix to analyze a new scale like Ionian b2 or or Ionian #5. See if you can come up with more!

I hope you enjoyed the 50 String Guitar and thank you for purchasing it! For more, search the web for videos from **The50StringGuitar**. To advance far beyond traditional scales look for my upcoming books (and practice, practice, practice).

Bryan Roberts

APPENDIX

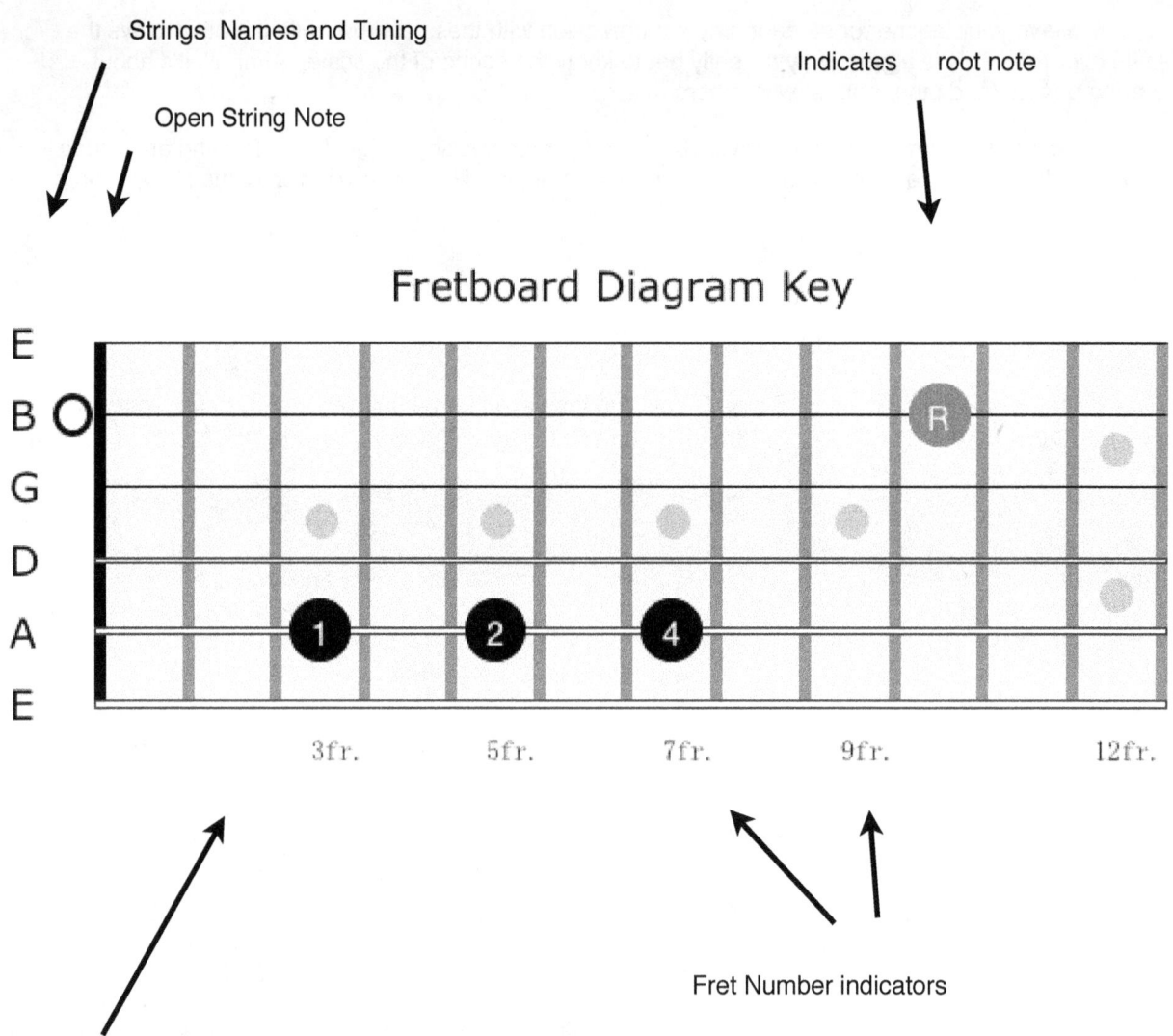

#'s indicates Scale Note Fingerings (1=index, 2=middle, 4=pinky) *OR* the Scale Degree in some charts

The 50 String Guitar

(20 strings of it anyway)

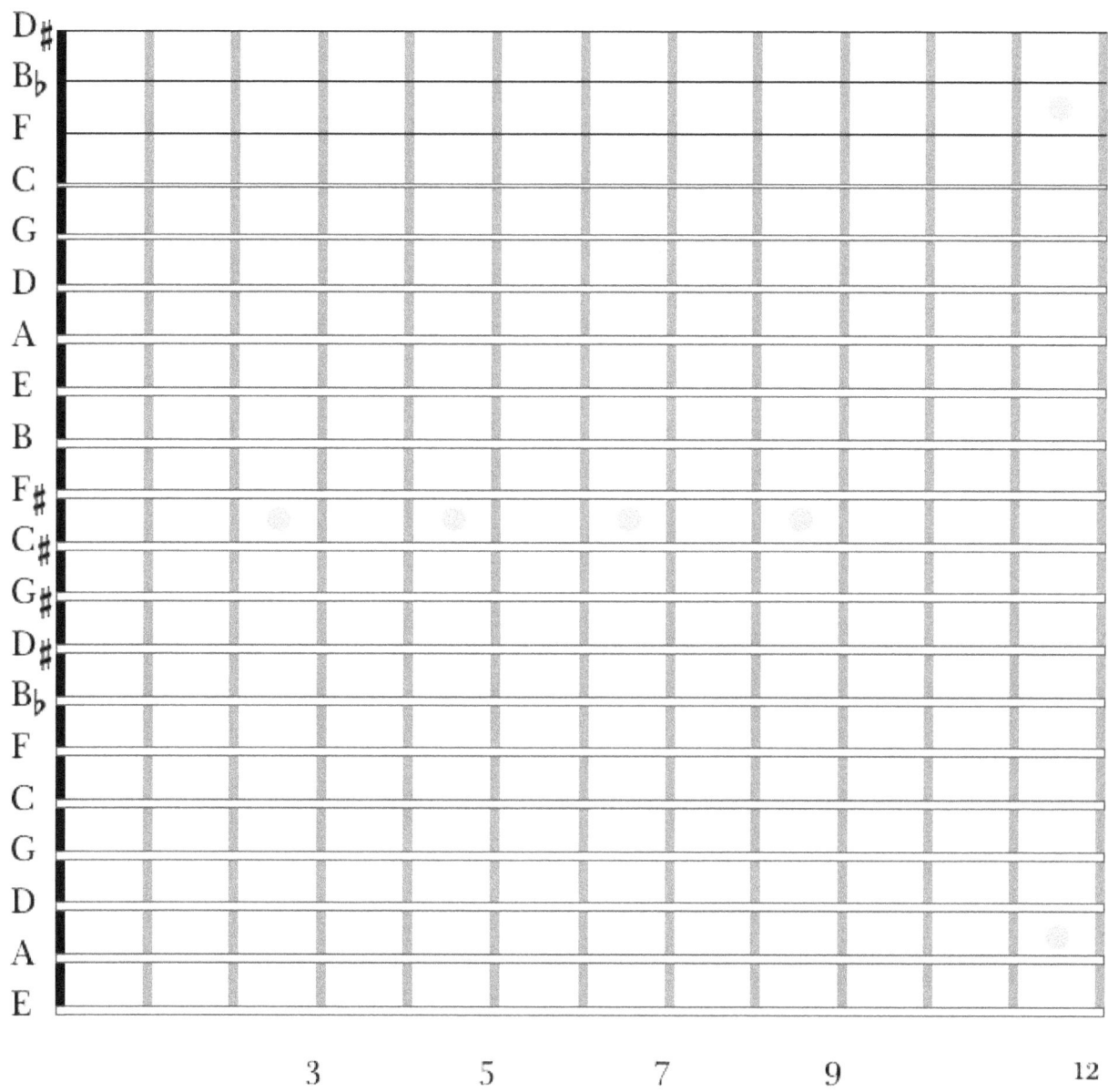

This guitar is a little different than yours. Not only does it have many more strings but it is tune entirely in perfect 4ths. This allows us to more easily see the full pattern of any scale as it ascends up the neck. Consider the the low E string of this guitar to be the same as yours. The difference comes at your B string and this is why you'll have to remember **The 2nd String Jump.** It is notable that D# is equivalent to Eb as G# ~ Ab, C# ~ Db, F# ~ Gb. See Circle of 5ths.

The Process
Running the Scales

Example 1

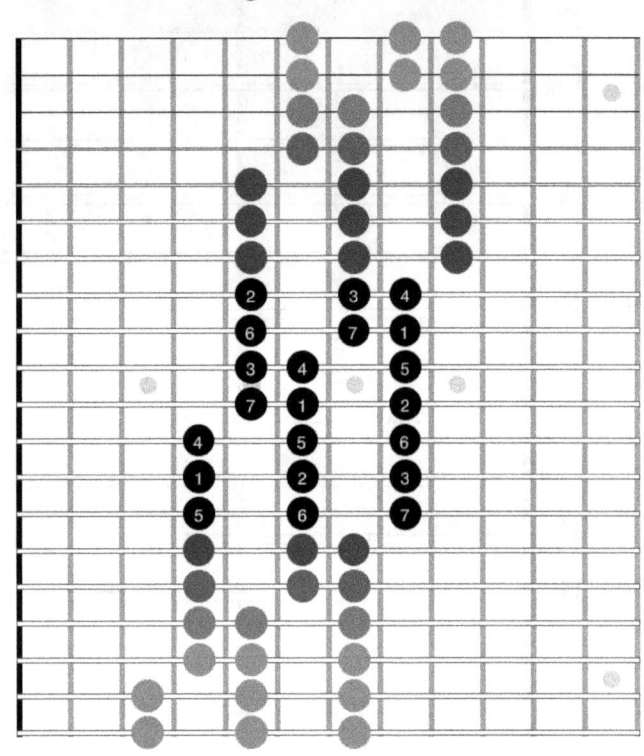

Major Scale

1. Choose your starting point on your guitar, e.g. Fret #1, String 6.
2. Choose the degree or mode of the scale with which you wish to begin, e.g. 5th (Mixolydian, 1st **Big One**.)
3. Follow the scale pattern on the 50 String Guitar diagram from the lower strings to the higher.
4. Do the **2nd String Jump!**
5. When you run out of strings, **repeat** the same basic shape that you played on string 1 in the same fret on string 6 and continue on with the pattern.

(For more help search the web for video by The50StringGuitar.)

Do this for any scale you wish to learn. For variation and different keys, start on different frets and even different strings. Remember where the 1 is! That note is the root note and tells you the key in which you are playing. Do it in reverse and even shift positions using the Modal Number!

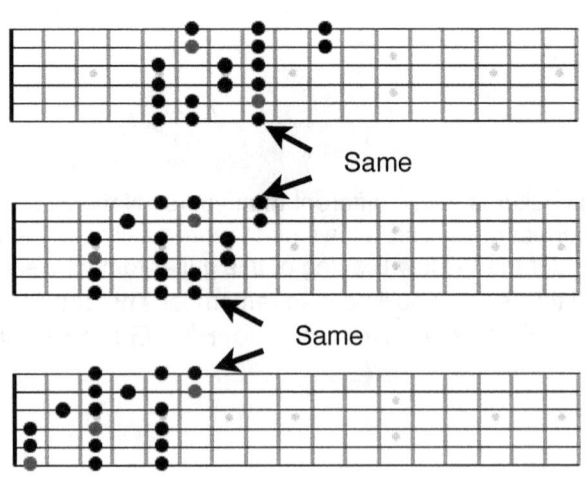

3 — This would be your third mode in the example above. Continue on up the neck.

2 — Your second mode will look like this. Notice that it begins where the first mode below ended.

1 — In the example above your first mode will look like this. F Mixolydian in the key of Bb.

Scale Comparison Chart

Major	Melodic Minor	Bebop Dominant	Bebop Major	Harmonic Minor	Harmonic Major
Ionian	Ionian b3	Ionian + #4th	Ionian + #5	Ionian #5	Ionian b6
Dorian	Dorian b2	Dorian + Δ3rd	Dorian + #4	Dorian #4	Dorian b5
Phrygian	Phrygian b1	Phrygian + Δ2	Phrygian + Δ3	Phrygian #3	Phrygian b4
Lydian	Lydian b7	Lydian + #1	Lydian + #2	Lydian #2	Lydian b3
		*Locrydian			
Mixolydian	Mixolydian b6	Mixolydian + Δ7th	Mixolydian + #1	Mixolydian #1	Mixolydian b2
			*Diminished Augmented		
Aeolian	Aeolian b5	Aeolian + Δ6th	Aeolian + Δ7	Aeolian #7	Aeolian b1
Locrian	Locrian b4	Locrian + p 5th	Locrian + Δ6	Locrian #6	Locrian b7

*These 8 note scales have an extra mode. 'Traditional' names are shown.

For fun see if you can identify and play other Ionian relatives like Ionian b2 or Ionian #2.

Super Theory Guy says - "The names don't tell me how the scales function! Melodic Minor should be Aeolian #6 #7!"

Super Player Guy replies - "The way I use them tells you how they function!"

Tradition View for Comparison

Am/C Major Pentatonic

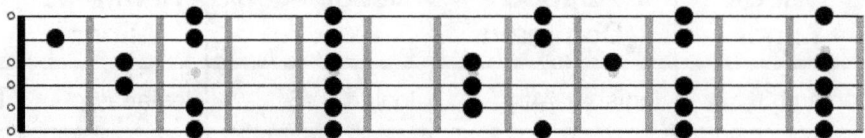

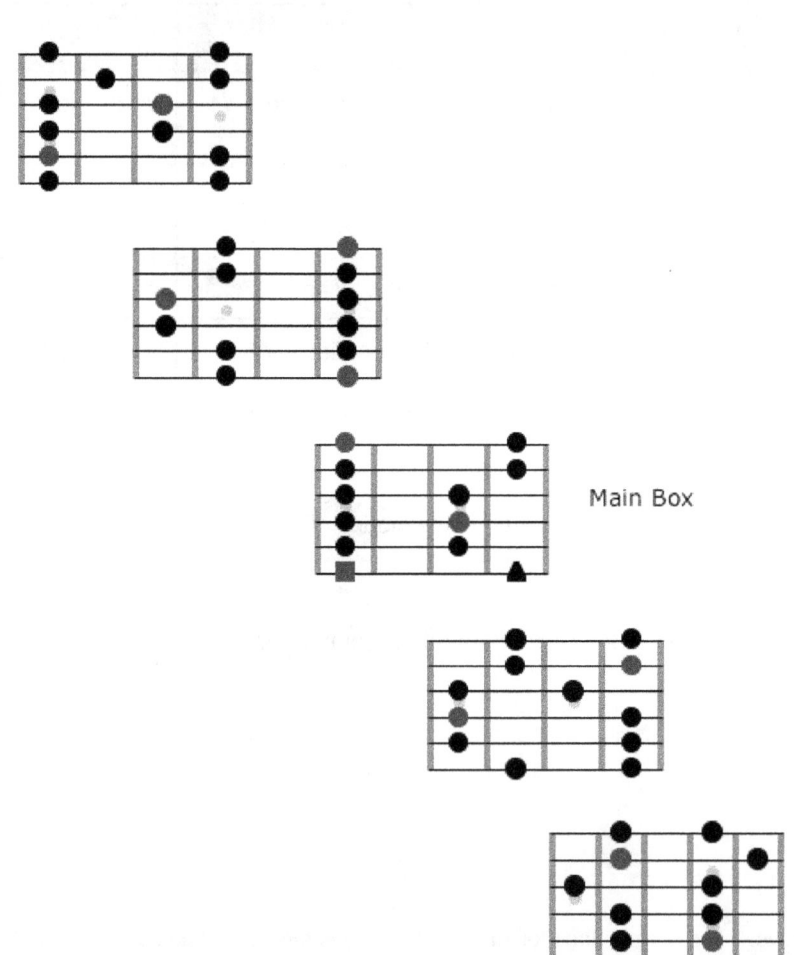

Main Box

C Major

CΔ7-Dm7-Em7-FΔ7-G7-Am7-Bm7b5

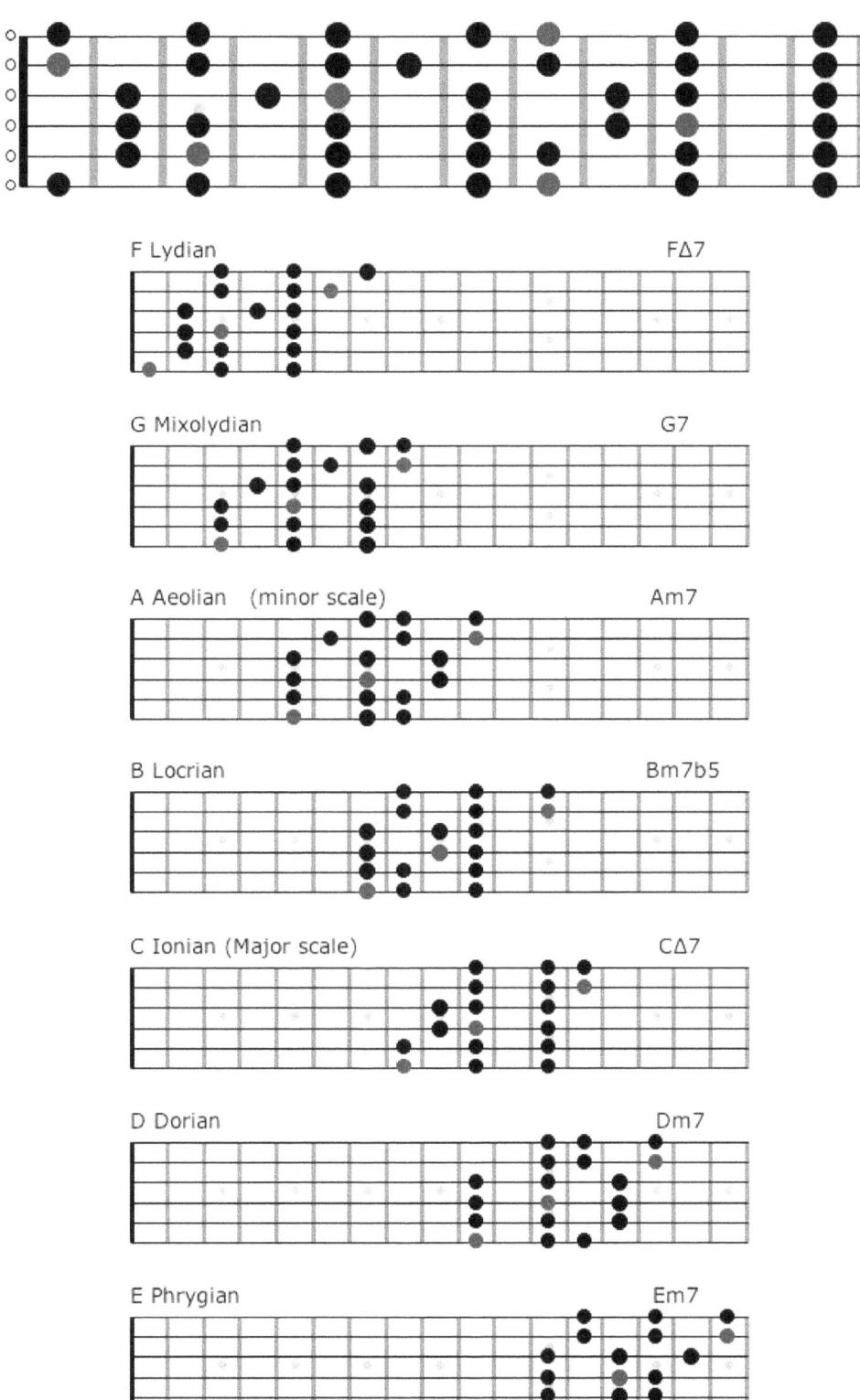

C Melodic Minor

CmΔ7-Dm7b9-EbΔ7#5-F7#11-G7b13-Am7b5#2-Balt.

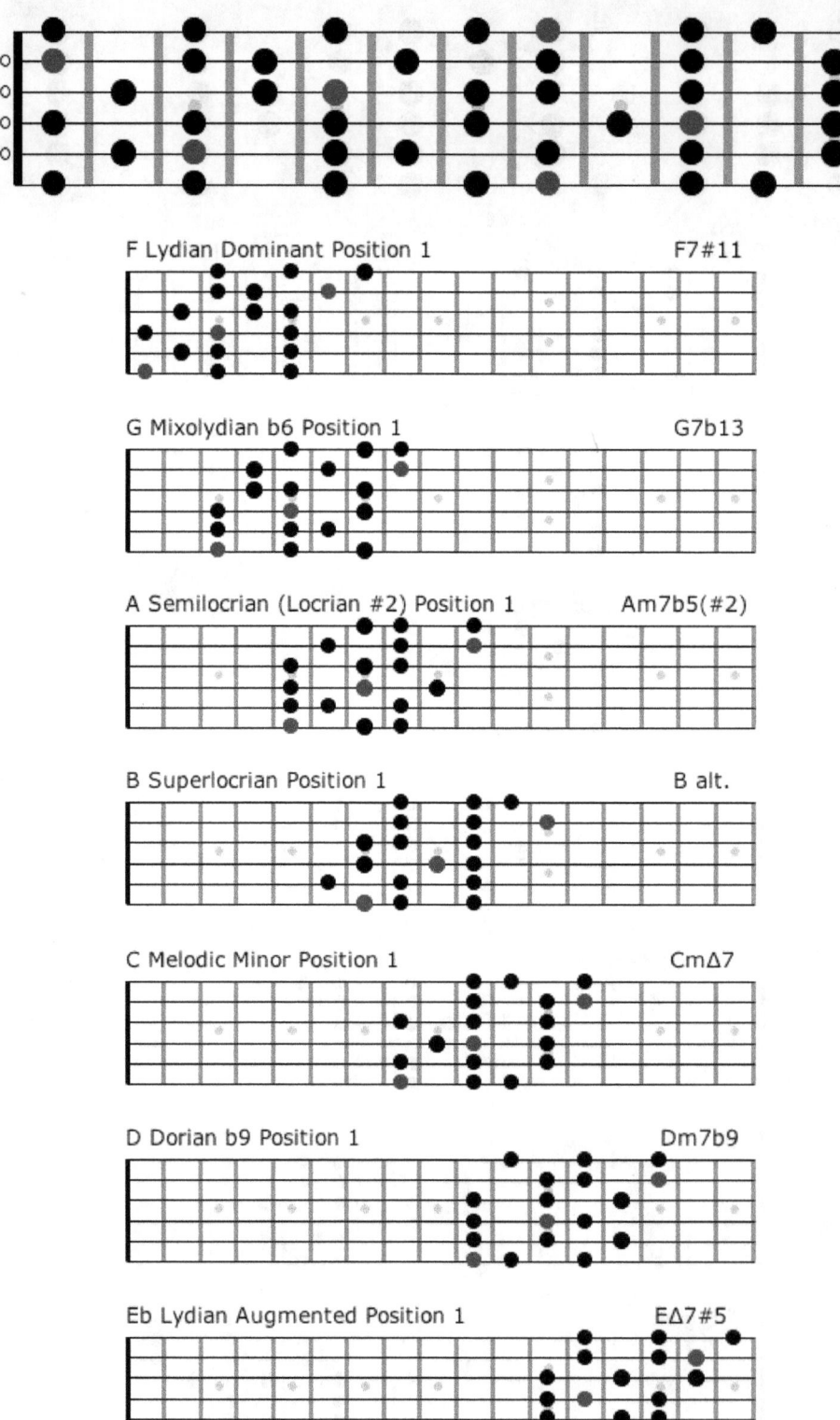

C Harmonic Minor

CmΔ7-Dm7b5-EbΔ7#5-Fm7#11-G7b9b13-AbΔ7#11-Bbim7

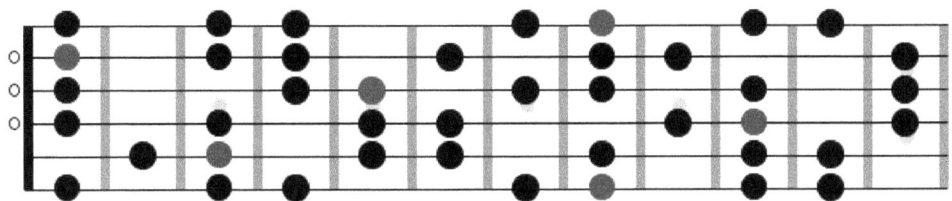

F Romanian (Dorian #11) Position 1
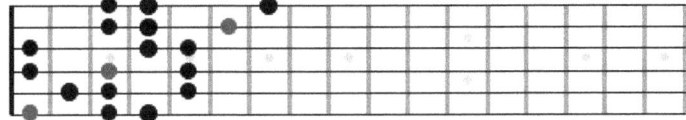

G Phrygian Dominant (Spanish Gypsy) Position 1
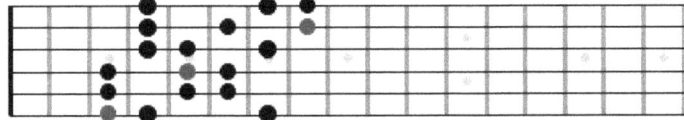

G# Lydian #2 Position 1
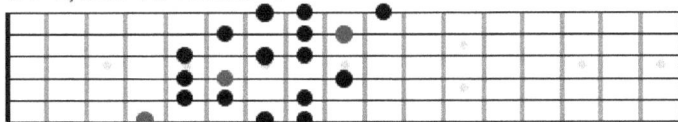

B Ultralocrian (Superlocrian bb7) Position 1
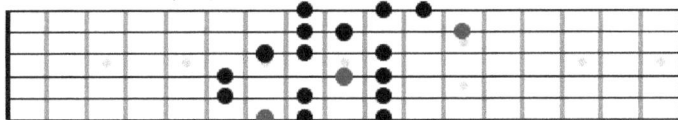

C Harmonic Minor Position 1
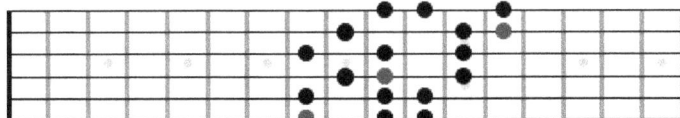

D Locrian #6 Position 1
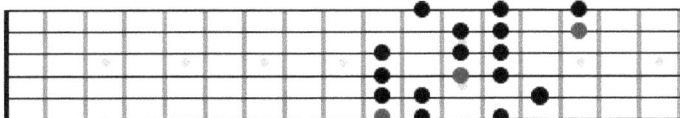

D# Ionian Augmented Position 1
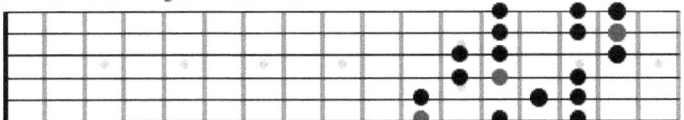

C Harmonic Major

CΔ7(b13)-Dm7b5-Em7(b11)ALT- FmΔ7(#11)-G7b9-AbΔ7Aug(#9)-Bdim

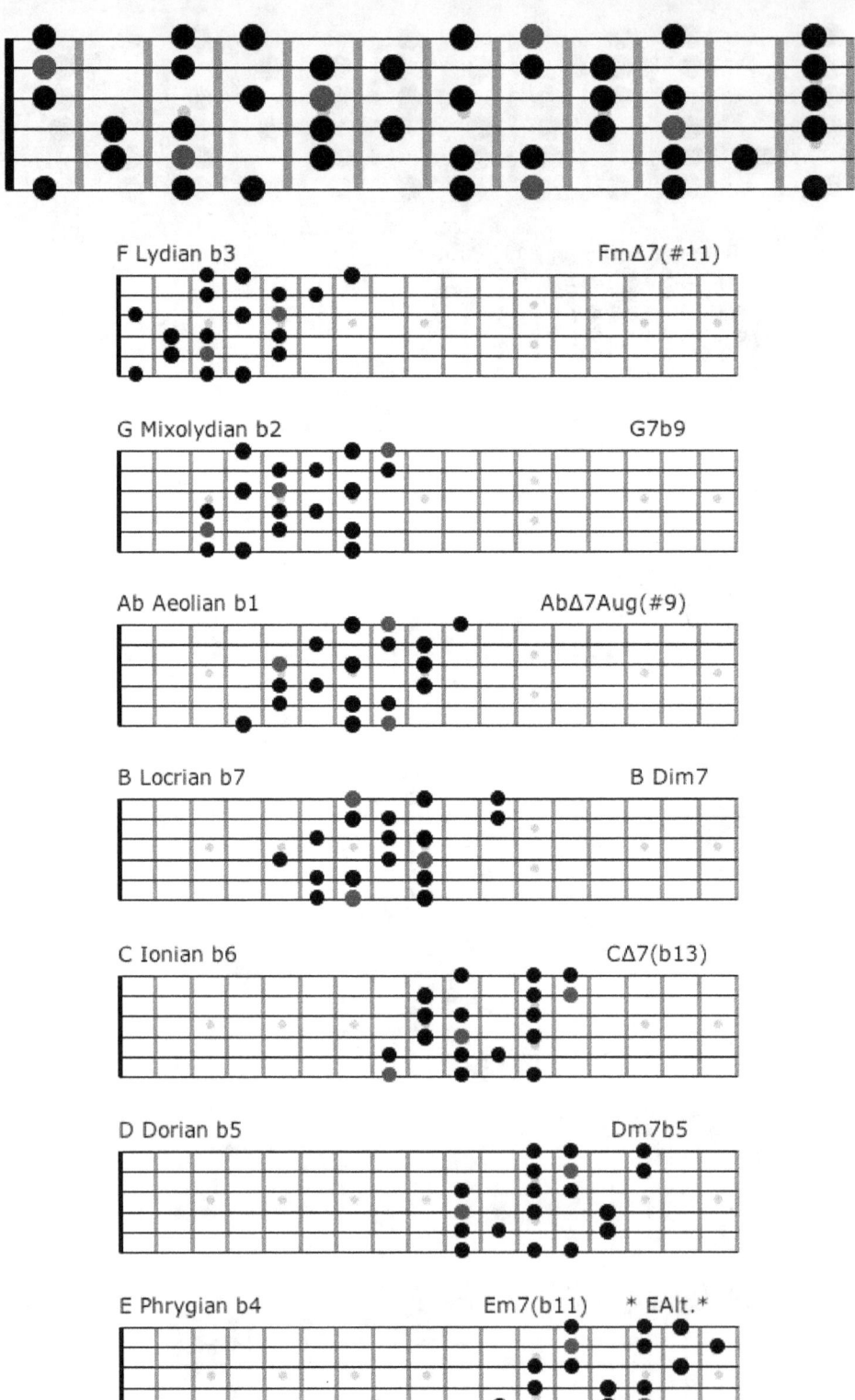

C Bebop Dominant

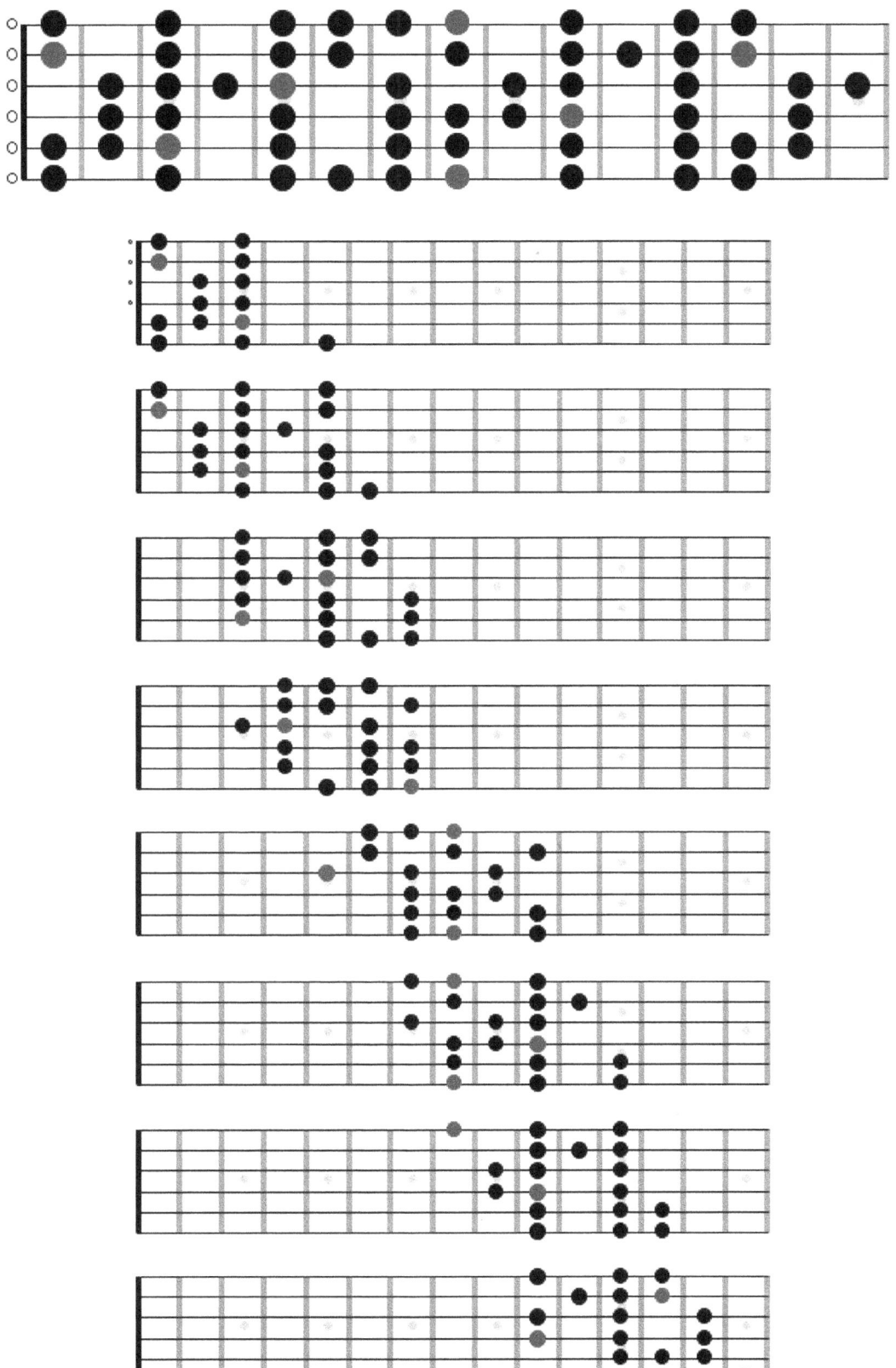

C Bebop Major

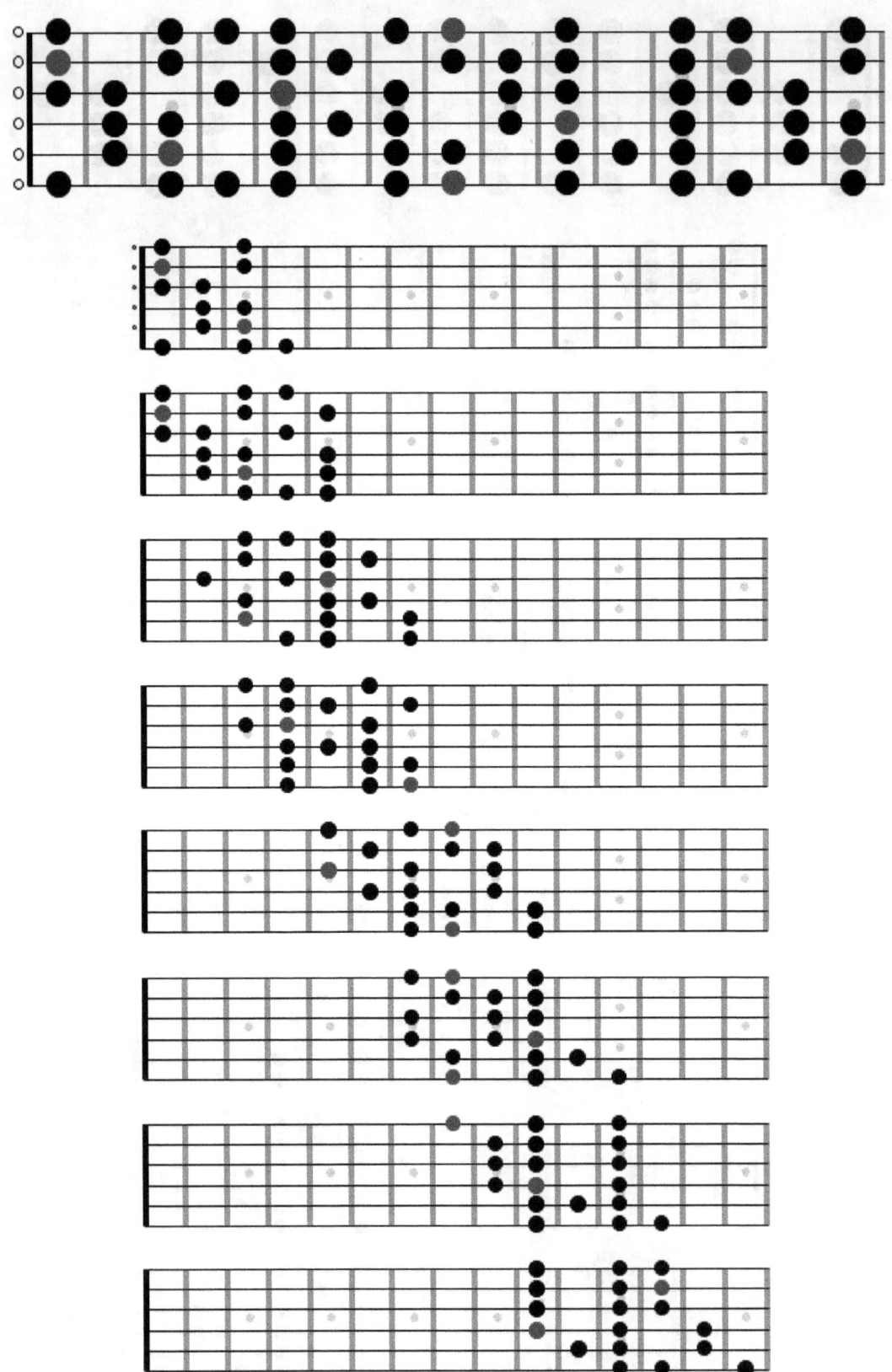

C W/H Diminished

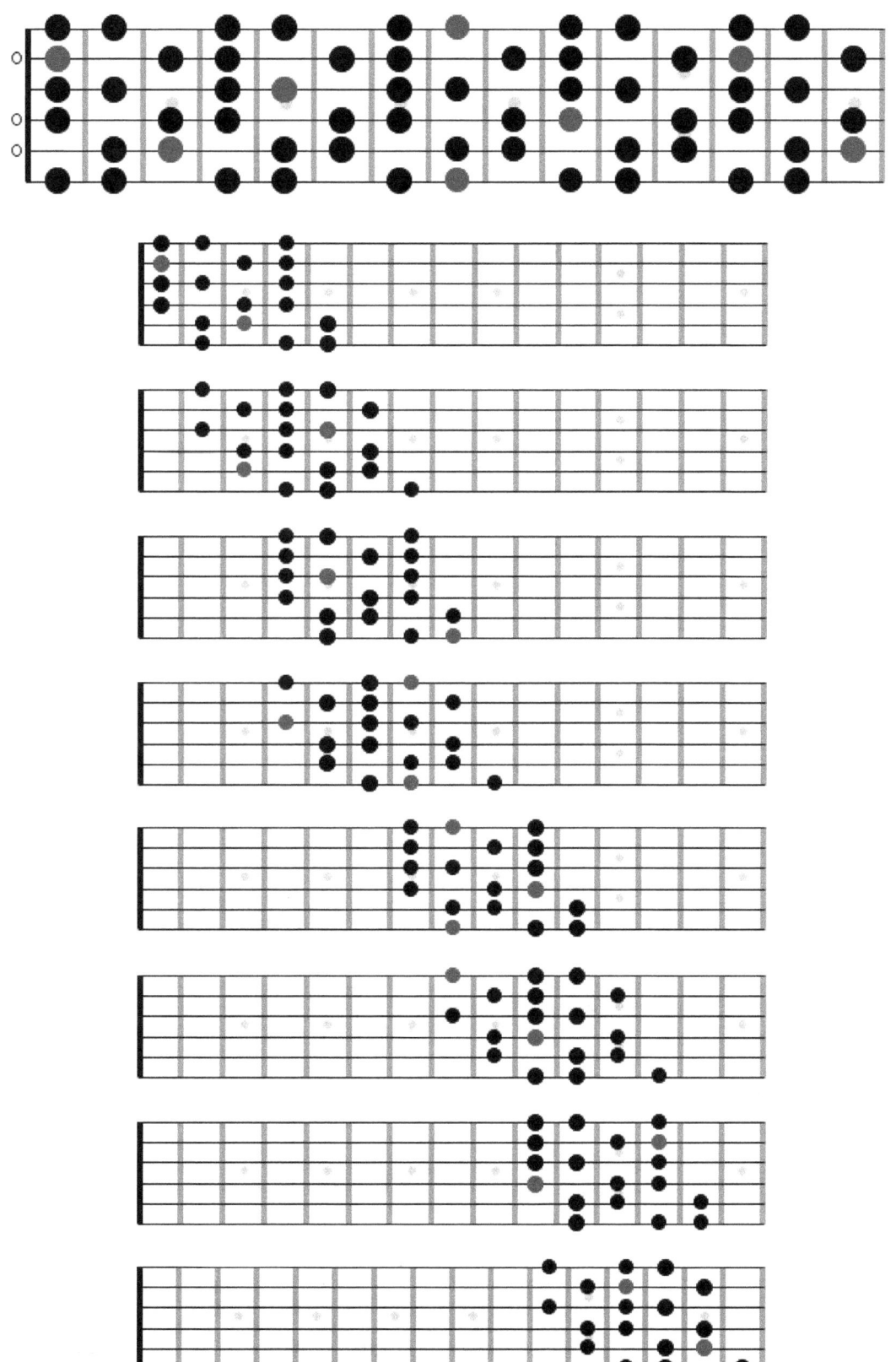

C Whole Tone

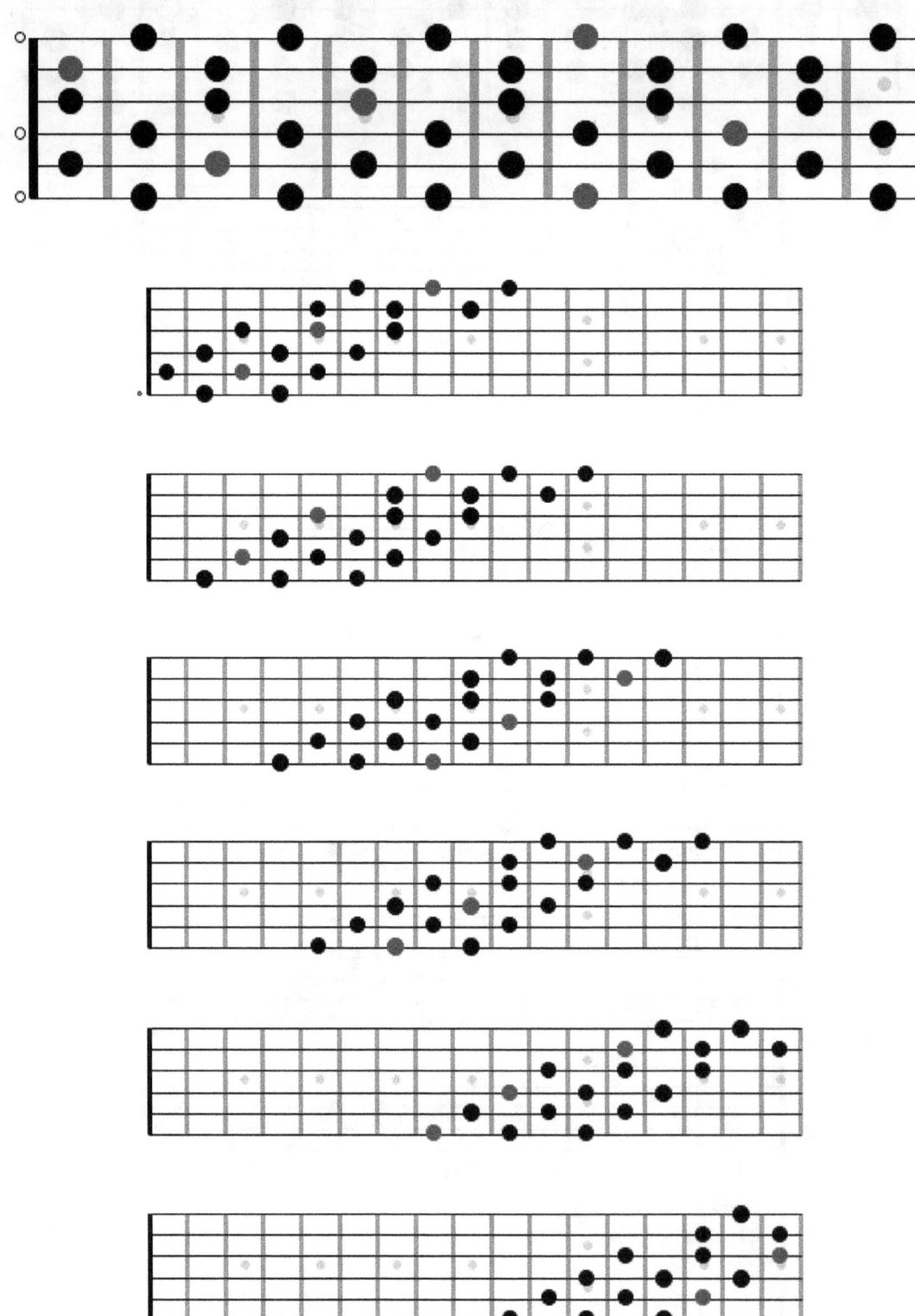

Notes

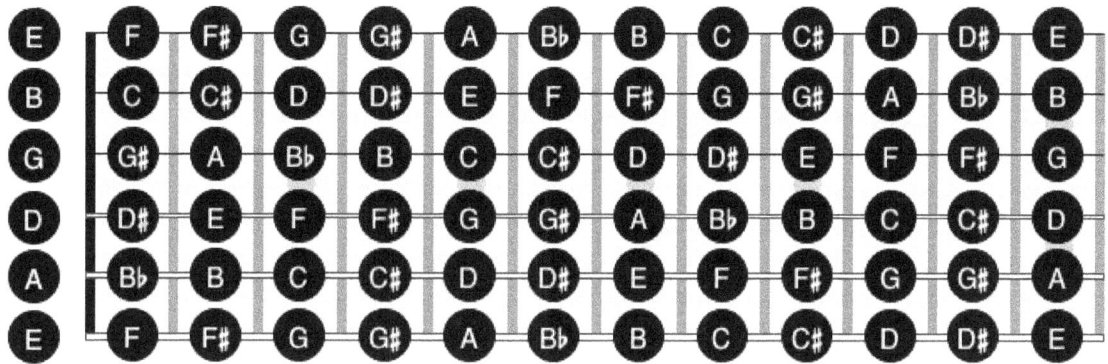

Don't try to memorize all of this. Just know the following...

Open Strings

1E 2B 3G 4D 5A 6E

Going up and down the neck B and C

and E and F are always beside each other.

\# = up one fret   b = down one fret

Knowing this you should be able to find any note on the guitar.

Yes F# is in the same spot as Gb just as G# is in the same spot as Ab etc..

(This information can also be used to tune your guitar.)

Interval Study/Reference

Know what is around you. R = Root Note

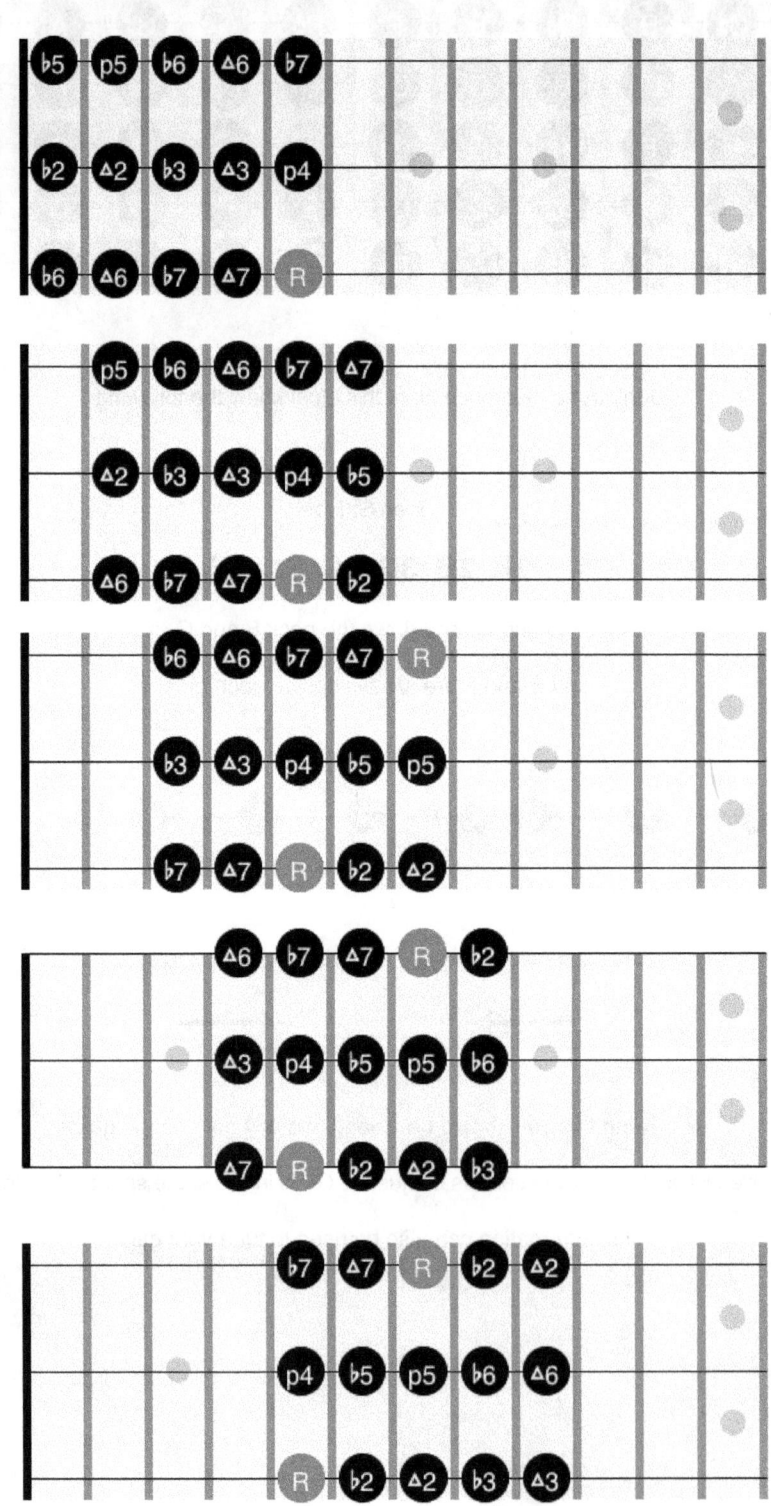

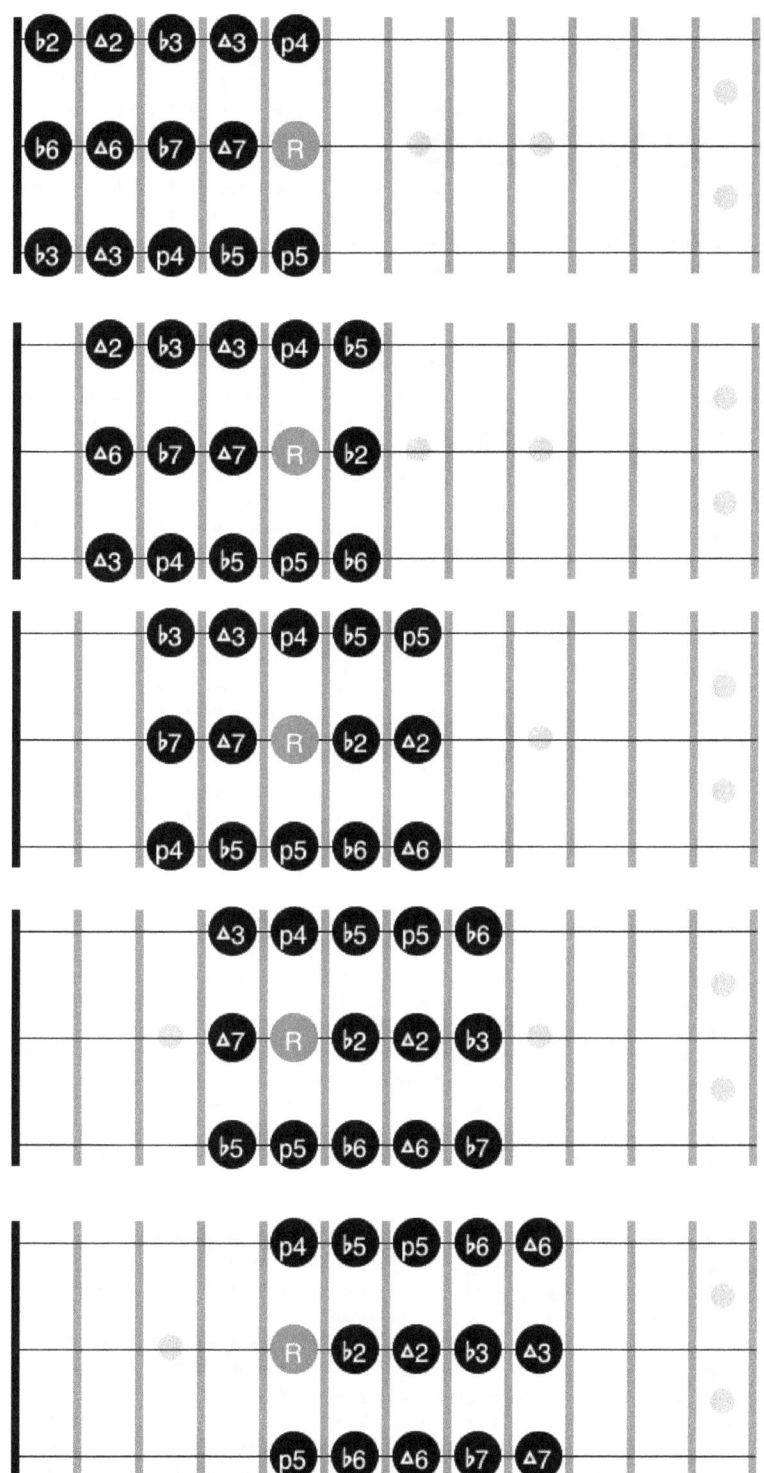

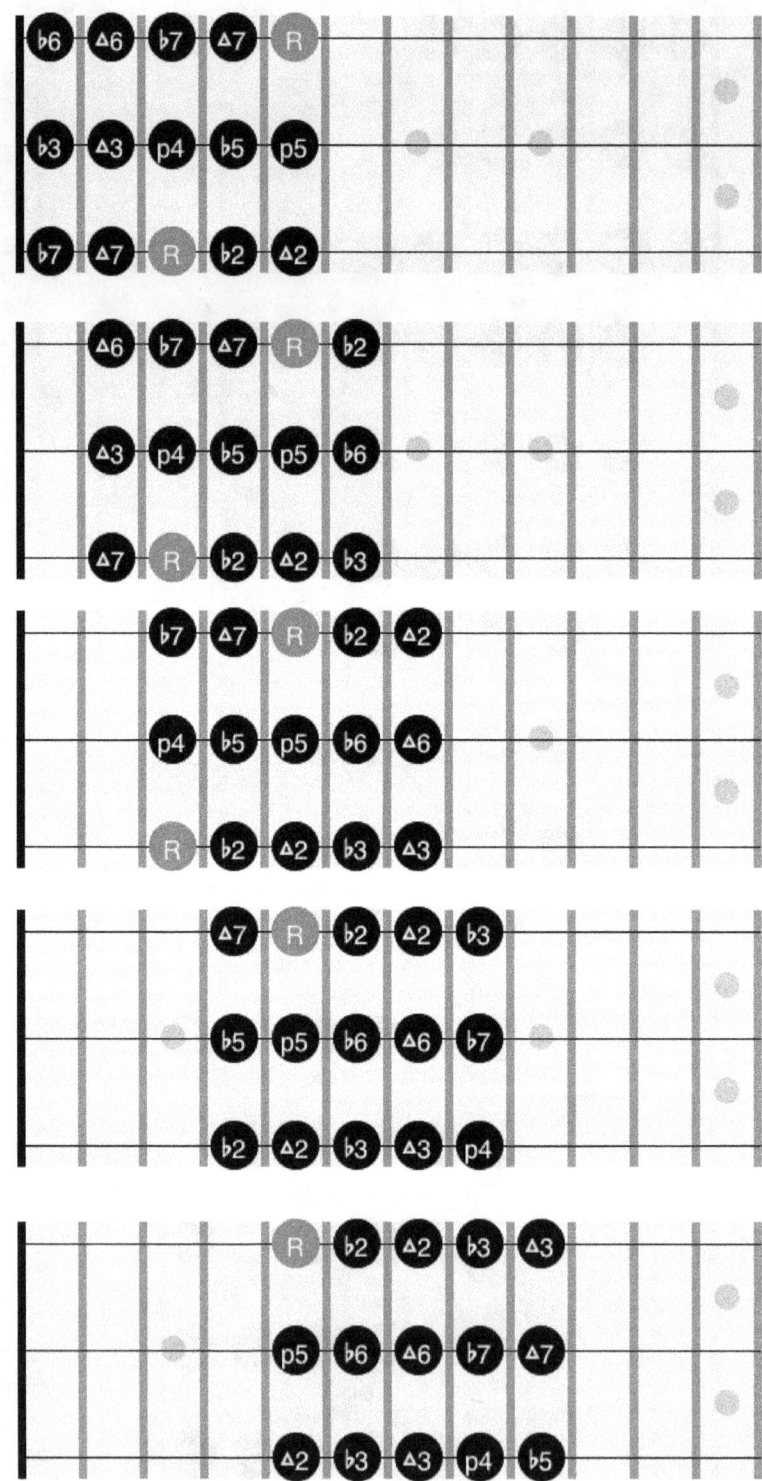

Blanks for Printing and Study

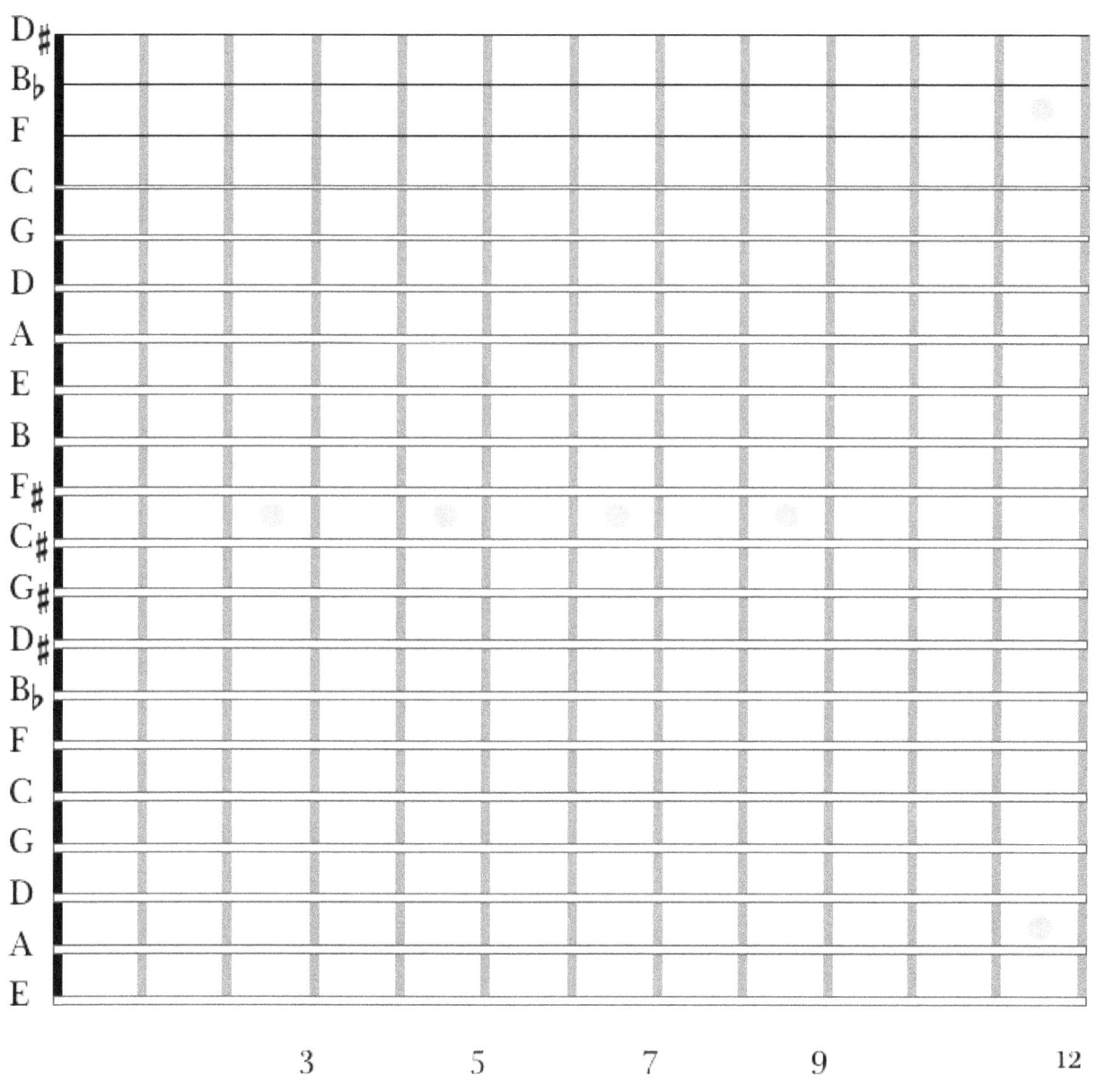

The 50 String Guitar by Bryan Roberts

www.ingramcontent.com/pod-product-compliance
Lightning Source LLC
Chambersburg PA
CBHW081258170426
43198CB00017B/2842